CAPE COD
—— AND THE ——
PORTLAND
GALE OF 1898

CAPE COD
—— AND THE ——
PORTLAND
GALE OF 1898

DON WILDING

THE
History
PRESS

Published by The History Press
Charleston, SC
www.historypress.com

First published 2023

Manufactured in the United States

ISBN 9781467151672

Library of Congress Control Number: 2022950034

In Loving Memory of

Harriet B. Wilding
June 24, 1930–September 18, 2021

Contents

Acknowledgements

This book would not have been possible without the help of a wide variety of friends, on and off Cape Cod.

John DeSousa at the Pilgrim Monument and Provincetown Museum; Bill Burke and Jill Ficarrotta at Cape Cod National Seashore; Rebekah Ambrose-Dalton at the William Brewster Nickerson Cape Cod History Archives of the Wilkens Library at Cape Cod Community College; Deb Rich at the Sandwich Town Archives, Sandwich Public Library; Eileen Seaboldt, Marca Daley and Patti Donohoe at the Eastham Historical Society; Don Stucke, Mary Everett-Patriquin and Elizabeth York at the Cape Cod Maritime Museum in Hyannis; Cape Cod Coast Guard historian Richard Boonisar; Lucy Loomis and the staff at Sturgis Library, Barnstable; Meg Costello and Mark Schmidt at the Falmouth Historical Society's Museums on the Green; Teresa Lamperti at the Brewster Historical Society; Joe Manas, Dave and Meri Hartford and the French Cable Station Museum in Orleans; Amy Andreasson at the Eldredge Public Library in Chatham; Michael Lach and the Harwich Conservation Trust; Katie Campbell at the Sandwich Glass Museum; Gene Guill and Tales of Cape Cod; Danielle Kovacs at the University of Massachusetts/ Amherst's Robert S. Cox Special Collections and University Archives Research Center; Pat Corcoran at the Dennis Historical Society's Dennis Maritime Museum in West Dennis; Bob Dwyer, Kate Roderick, Teresa Izzo and everyone at the Cape Cod Museum of Natural History; Bob Seay, Shirley Weber, Debbie Abbott, Deborah Ullman, Laura Roskos and everyone at the Nauset Fellowship (UU), Chapel in the Pines, Eastham; Dave Drabkin; Glenn and Sheila Mott; and Jon March.

Also, many thanks for the virtual visuals and tidbits of information from Ben Kettlewell, Lisa King and Salvador Vasques, as well as to Donna Tunney at the *Cape Codder* newspaper in Orleans, where some of the material in this book saw its first printed form in my "Shore Lore" columns.

I'd also like to extend thanks to the dozens of organizations on Cape Cod and across New England that have hosted my Cape Cod history lectures since 2001.

There are many good people who are no longer with us who contributed to this effort in one way, shape or form over the years, more than they would ever know: Nan Turner Waldron, George and Rosemary Abbott, George Rongner, Noel Beyle, Jim Owens, Phil Ryder and Terri Rae Smith.

Finally, I could never have accomplished any of this without the love and support of my son, Matt Wilding; and my wife, Nita Wilding. Much love to you both.

INTRODUCTION

For hundreds of years, the New England region has long held a fascination with the storms lashing its coastlines. Every generation has some sort of recollection, a benchmark weather event, that stirs the senses and memories.

Alton H. Blackington, a mid-twentieth-century storyteller known for his *Yankee Yarns*, was no exception. During his childhood, his mother's opinion of what was the worst meteorological monster always came through loud and clear whenever the barometer dropped. Peering out the frosty window, her observation was something that stuck in the mind of her author-to-be offspring:

> *"'Twas just such a night as this that the* Portland *went down!" The way she said it would give me goose-pimples, and I still shudder on wild winter nights when the surf flies and the wind howls.*

"When the *Portland* went down." It's an expression that always accompanies any tales about "the *Portland* Gale" of November 26 and 27, 1898. The Thanksgiving weekend "northeaster" set the bar for storm severity for the first half of the twentieth century and beyond. Not until the "Blizzard of '78" plowed its way through southeastern New England in early February 1978 was there a weather event that even began to slightly nudge the "Great Gale of 1898" off its lofty perch of New England winter storm supremacy. In its report for Truro on December 13, 1898, the *Chatham Monitor* said that "men who remember the gale of 1851, when Minot's Light went down, declared that this latest visitor far exceeded in violence that of '51."

The storm was dubbed "the *Portland* Gale" after the paddle steamer *Portland*, making its daily run from Boston to its namesake city in Maine, was lost in the storm, claiming an estimated 192 lives after sinking over Stellwagen Bank. Overall, an estimated 456 people died at sea during the storm. Sylvester Baxter noted in the November 1899 edition of *Scribner's Magazine* that the storm's death toll was "more than were killed in battle on our side in the recent war with Spain."

At sea, wind speeds surpassed one hundred miles per hour, while the waves crested at sixty feet, higher than the *Portland*'s smokestacks, according to a 2002 report from the Associated Press. A total of 141 vessels were lost, including 40 from Cape Cod. The harbors at Vineyard Haven and Provincetown saw the pileups of dozens of ships. Eric Fisher, chief meteorologist at WBZ-TV in Boston, noted in his book *Mighty Storms of New England* that it was "the most destructive year in the history of New England shipwrecks" and that the storm was "responsible for seventy percent of all vessels lost." The *Boston Sunday Post* reported that "during Fiscal Year 1897, there were 394 disasters nationwide. During the Portland Gale storm, there were 187 wrecks."

The storm was the configuration of two areas of low pressure that rapidly intensified south of Nantucket. A few days later, newspapers near and far were still busy gathering the facts, but it was clear right away that this storm was one for the record books. The November 29, 1898 edition of the *Harwich Independent* reported:

> *The oldest inhabitant has been scratching his head to recall a storm that has happened within his remembrance as severe as that of Saturday night and Sunday. It is safe to say no storm in recent years has equaled it in severity and widespread disaster.*

At the tip of the Cape, Provincetown was among the areas worst hit, with dozens of ships piling up in its usually safe harbor. All but one of Provincetown's wharves was destroyed. Just to the south of Falmouth, on the island of Martha's Vineyard, a similar scene was unfolding in Vineyard Haven Harbor.

The storm continued to be the standard for Cape Cod storms for most of the twentieth century. Thirty years later, in his Cape Cod literary classic *The Outermost House*, Henry Beston, writing of the great storm of February 19 and 20, 1927, noted, "They say here that it was the worst gale known on

The Provincetown Harbor waterfront saw extensive damage during the storm of November 26–27, 1898. *From the collections of the Pilgrim Monument & Provincetown Museum.*

the outer Cape since the *Portland* went down with all hands on that terrible November night in '98."

In this book, the objective is to take you, the reader, across Cape Cod on that fateful weekend in 1898 and share the stories of how the heroic locals stood up to the storm and aided in the recovery from its impact. The narrative is woven together largely from newspaper reports, magazines, books, interviews and details from the 1899 annual report of the U.S. Life-Saving Service.

The tragedy of the steamer *Portland* was the headline story, but the *Portland* Gale left the region paralyzed for several days. For many weeks, the sea gave up but a fraction of the *Portland*'s dead on the Cape's beaches. Still more Cape Cod mariners went to sea and never returned, caught in the gale's evil clutches. The men of the U.S. Life-Saving Service faced challenges they never dreamed of. It was a major disaster that was felt around the country and the world. Cape Cod historian William Quinn explained its impact to the *Standard-Times* of New Bedford in 1998:

> *If you want to relate it to today's news, you might compare it to TWA Flight 800, when all those people had to go to Long Island to try and identify those bodies. There was the same thing on Cape Cod. There was a lot of sorrow.*

In 1928, Douglas H. Shepherd, keeper of Wood End Light in Provincetown, made the observation of how the tale of the *Portland* Gale endured—and continues to do so to this day:

> *It was, indeed, a storm, this gale of '98. And there were many old timers left who are still willing and eager to settle down and begin their story: "It was in '98, when the* Portland *went down...."*

A Meteorological
Monster Emerges

Shortly the sun's brilliance becomes slightly dulled.
An almost invisible "smur" thickens; a light air comes in from the east,
and the barometer starts to drop. Such a day, known as a "weather breeder"
on Cape Cod, means a real easterly is in the offing.
—*Wyman Richardson,* The House on Nauset Marsh

All was relatively quiet along the coast of Massachusetts on the morning of November 26, 1898. From Boston to Cape Cod, those who made their living on the water were busy in their usual routines. But they all knew that something wasn't right.

At the Monomoy Life-Saving Station just south of Chatham, surfman Ben Eldredge "was outside doing a bit of washing." Still relatively new to the lifesaving business, he glanced out over the water. "There was a queer blue light over everything," Eldredge recalled for the *Cape Cod Standard-Times* in 1967. His fellow surfmen, he said, "were strangely quiet…not a joke among them. Even the gulls were hanging around the flats and not screaming."

Alfred F. Nickerson of Chatham had a similar vision aboard *Coal Barge No. 1* of the Consolidated Coal Company, which was headed from Baltimore to Boston carrying 1,600 tons of coal. "It had been just as smooth as glass all afternoon, but the sky looked awful funny," Nickerson recalled for the *Cape Codder* newspaper of Orleans in 1947. "It had a shiny, glassy look."

Reverend S.S. Nickerson of the Boston Seamen's Friend Society said that "the sky was leaden-deep and murky" at Chatham Light about 6:30 p.m.

The storm of November 26–27, 1898, became known as "the *Portland* Gale" after 192 lives were lost on the steamer *Portland* after departing Boston. *Author's collection.*

Saturday, according to George Wiseman's *They Kept the Lower Lights Burning*. "Not a cat's paw on the water. The sea was calm. Like a tiger it was resting for a plunge that should destroy life."

Sylvester Baxter summed up the situation for *Scribner's Magazine* in November 1899: "The air was murky and ominously still, and was filled with the penetrating chill that meant snow, much snow. Something unusual was manifestly impending, but nobody dreamed what was really at hand." In the words of Benjamin Haines of Sandwich, in a letter to the Pratt family, "it was one of the evilest nights we ever experienced."

In Boston, Hollis Blanchard of the Portland Steamship Company was making his regular visit to the National Weather Bureau office to check in on the latest forecast. E.B. Rideout, a longtime meteorologist for WEEI radio in Boston, became well acquainted with the Boston Weather Bureau team during the years after the storm and recalled his conversations with them about the *Portland* Gale in for *Yankee Magazine* in 1966.

Blanchard, the captain of the paddle steamer *Portland*, was planning out his appointed 7:00 p.m. run from India Wharf to Portland, Maine. Blanchard was well acquainted with Chief Meteorologist John W. Smith and his team. The Weather Bureau's *Monthly Weather Review*, issued in January 1899, summed up the morning situation:

> *A storm center occupied lower Michigan, and an area of high barometer covered New England. A closer scrutiny of the reports will show evidence of a cyclonic wind circulation along the south Atlantic coast.*

Portland captain Hollis Blanchard was a frequent visitor to the Weather Bureau office in Boston. He checked in with the meteorologists there on the morning of November 26, 1898. *Library of Congress.*

Blanchard watched as Smith drew his map, taking note of the disturbance over Michigan. "It looks bad," the meteorologist said.

Smith's worst fears would be confirmed. According to Weather Bureau data, the Michigan storm center advanced to Pittsburgh, Pennsylvania, by noon, and the southern storm had deepened rapidly and moved to a position off Cape Hatteras, North Carolina. By 3:00 p.m., the centers had united off Norfolk, Virginia, and by the 8:00 p.m. report, the center of disturbance had deepened and was located off the New Jersey coast. At this point, Blanchard and the *Portland* had just left Boston.

William U. Swan, a longtime Associated Press reporter, detailed the storm's development, "somewhere south of Nantucket," for *Cape Cod Magazine* in 1921:

> *Like all storms in this part of the world, it drew into its deepening vortex, dry, cold winds from the north and west, and warm, damp winds from the south and east; all these wind being sucked into that vortex spirally, the center whirling around in the opposite directions to the hands of a clock. At the same time that it whirled about like a dust storm or an eddy in a city street, it had a movement of its own about north, northeast.*

During the day on Saturday, Swan reported that the storm tripled in size, growing from about thirty miles to one hundred miles wide, while wind speeds increased as the storm churned toward Cape Cod. Eric Fisher of WBZ-TV in Boston noted in his book *Mighty Storms of New England* that this "was the classic rapid intensification of a nor'easter, or bombogenesis. This occurs when then sea-level pressure falls at least twenty-four millibars in twenty-four hours."

Barometers across the coasts of southern New England plummeted. By midnight, Boston's pressure had dropped to 29.44 inches, according to historian Edward Rowe Snow. Captain Albert Bragg of the steamer *Horatio Hall*, which survived its journey through the stormy seas off the outer Cape during the early morning hours

Captain Hollis Blanchard of the steamer *Portland* was warned that "it looks bad" by Chief Meteorologist John W. Smith of the Weather Bureau prior to the ship's departure. *Eastham Historical Society.*

of November 27, reported a reading of 29.08 inches. On Martha's Vineyard, The *Vineyard Gazette* reported a reading of 28.9 inches at 3:00 a.m. on Sunday morning.

Weather conditions began to rapidly deteriorate over the region by ten o'clock Saturday night. Historian Al Snow recalled in 1961 that, in Orleans, "the storm began with wind gusts, then came heavy rain, thunder and lightning, then sleet. After nightfall came the howling blizzard and snow." The *Harwich Independent* reported that "in the early hours of Sunday morning this northeast gale increased to almost cyclone force and raged." Similar conditions were reported on Martha's Vineyard—"at about 3 o'clock Sunday morning the wind was blowing with hurricane force," the *Vineyard Gazette* reported. During the rescue effort by Life-Saving Service of the *Albert L. Butler* on Provincetown's back shore, surfman Bert Bangs recalled, by way of *Provincetown Advocate* columnist Bossy McGady in 1971, what he remembered most "were the awful streaks of lightning and crash of thunder above the roar of the storm."

In North Truro, the storm's wrath was felt at Highland Light, which was the first beacon established on the Cape. Isaac M. Small, the Boston Chamber of Commerce marine agent, wrote, "[S]uch was the force of this hurricane of wind that every window pane on the ocean side of our

Most of the windows at the Highland Light signal station were blown in and smashed by winds of one hundred miles per hour. *Cape Cod National Seashore.*

house, the signal station at Highland Light, was blown in and smashed into a thousand fragments."

The storm continued to rage for several hours, especially in the area of Provincetown. The *Provincetown Advocate* summarized the storm's activity:

> *The late gale began with wind almost due east and spits of snow almost 8 p.m. Saturday evening last. From 8 p.m. until nearly 10 p.m., the breeze was not unusually violent, but after that time the wind increased by leaps and bounds and at 2 a.m. Sunday morning was exceptionally boisterous. Then it increased to hurricane force and until 4 a.m. was without exception the most forceful wind experienced here in a lifetime. From 4 a.m. Sunday morning until 6 p.m. that day a hurricane prevailed.*

While the storm was not officially classified as a tropical cyclone, it did take on the characteristics of such a weather event when it developed an eye. William U. Swan made gave this report for the Associated Press:

> *The center passed over the Cape, which is generally agreed to have been about 9:30 on Sunday morning. The sky at that time over the stretch between Chatham and Barnstable cleared off entirely and the wind died out. Fifteen minutes after it was blowing hard from the north.*

In his summary for *Cape Cod Magazine* in December 1921, Swan wrote:

> *It was noted at Sandwich that during the forenoon of the 27th, the weather suddenly cleared, the sun came out and the wind ceased completely, although the horizon in all directions was massed with flying clouds. Half an hour later the storm had set in again.*

The brief break in the storm may have also provided an opportunity for eyewitness accounts of the steamer *Portland* off Provincetown on the morning of the twenty-seventh. Captain Michael Hogan, trying to reach Provincetown Harbor aboard the fishing vessel *Ruth M. Martin*, repeatedly claimed to have spotted the distressed steamer before severe weather resumed.

It was around this time that the crew of the Race Point Life-Saving Station in Provincetown heard what they thought could be the *Portland*, according to the *Boston Daily Advertiser*:

> *As to the storm center, the lifesavers at Race Point are the only ones who tell of that sudden lull in the gale during which they so plainly heard the blasts from the distressed steamer. It was if the furious tempest had ceased entirely for the space of breath and then as suddenly began again with renewed violence.*

In Truro, Lillian Small, wife of the Boston Chamber of Commerce ship observer Isaac M. Small, claimed to have seen the *Portland* from her home near Highland Light during the lull.

The *Harwich Independent* reported that the storm produced "three rainbows, two in the north and one in the south, and a tempest."

Alfred F. Nickerson of Chatham, who earlier had noted the early warning signs of foul weather on Saturday morning, ended up being rescued near Boston Harbor during the storm. His take on the storm's intensity was simple: "When she started to blow—boy!"

Further complicating matters was that November 27 was the full moon. Listed here are the lunar and tide charts from the 1898 *Old Farmer's Almanac*:

> *November, Eleventh Month:*
> *Full moon, 27th day, 11 h. 39 m., evening, W.*

> *Full Sea, Boston:*
> *Nov. 26—Morn., 9-3/4; Even., 10-1/4.*

Lillian Small, shown here in a sketch from the *Boston Post*, said that she spotted the *Portland* from her home near Highland Light. *Author's collection.*

Nov. 27—Morn., 10-1/2; Even., 11.
Nov. 28—Morn., 11-1/4; Even., 11-3/4.

Combine all these conditions and mariners at sea, along with those along Eastern Seaboard shores, were in peril like never before. As the U.S. Life-Saving Service noted in its Annual Report for 1899:

> *No such appalling calamity has occurred anywhere near by the coasts of the United States, or on the shore, for almost half a century, and it is doubtful whether there has been within the same period a coastal storm of such Titanic power.*

THE *TITANIC* OF NEW ENGLAND

They have heard evil tidings; they are fainthearted.
There is sorrow on the sea; it cannot be quiet.
—Jeremiah 49:23

Over the years, the *Portland* became known as the "*Titanic* of New England," in reference to the British passenger liner that sank in the Atlantic Ocean in 1912, claiming more than 1,500 lives.

The mysteries of the steamship *Portland*'s demise over Thanksgiving weekend of 1898 are many. One of them, no doubt, is why Captain Hollis Blanchard decided to venture out in the first place, even though he knew a winter storm was fast approaching. Whatever the answer is, history has not been kind to Blanchard. But is that justified?

"It [was] clearly a case of bad judgment and disobedience of orders on his part," J.F. Liscomb, general manager of the Portland Steamship Company, told reporters the week following the disaster. "Captain Blanchard should not have left Boston. I can't understand why he did. It was an awful mistake."

Blanchard, fifty-five, became the *Portland*'s commander in April 1898, as several newspapers reported after the steamer's voyage. The Portland, Maine resident was a family man and highly respected in maritime circles. He was also considered to be in line to be the company's next commodore.

The *Portland* was built in Bath, Maine, in 1890. The steamer measured 250 feet in length, was 15 feet deep and 42 feet in beam and 1,517 tons net

"Everybody in Boston knew the *Portland*. She was an institution," reported the *New York Journal*. The steamer was known for its luxurious accommodations. *Cape Cod Maritime Museum.*

burden. The ship even enjoyed celebrity status, according to the November 30, 1898 edition of the *New York Journal*:

> *Everybody in Boston knew the* Portland*. She was an institution. Those who had not taken a trip in her had nearly all been on board her at one time or another. Although a paddle wheeler, with all the ton-hamper of decks and staterooms common in river boats, she was believed to be a thoroughly staunch ocean-going craft.*

The *Portland* was scheduled to leave for its namesake city at 7:00 p.m. Weather forecasts were calling for a developing storm to hit eastern Massachusetts that night. The midday weather update called for the following conditions in Massachusetts:

> *Heavy snow tonight. Sunday, snow followed by clearing and much colder, southeasterly, shifting to northeasterly gales tonight, and northwesterly gales by Sunday.*

Blanchard's decision to set sail has been considered careless by many, but there was a time that he was considered the opposite. Blanchard was a regular visitor to the Boston Weather Bureau office, where he struck up a friendship with the officer in charge. Blanchard became well read in all things weather. The company also became aware that these daily weather sessions had become highly influential in shaping his decisions.

E.B. Rideout, a longtime weather forecaster for WEEI radio in Boston, was mentored by the same Weather Bureau meteorologists. The steamers were competing with the railroad for not only passengers but also freight. Cancelations due to weather could result in significant financial loss for the steamship company. Rideout shared what they told him about Blanchard for the *New England Guide* in 1966:

> *There came a day when Blanchard was called "on the carpet" and was told that he was really being too cautious. It is quite evident that during the conversation the financial problem was taken up and he was told to take greater risks.*

Blanchard was reported to believe that he could beat the incoming storm to Portland. "There were a great number of passengers who spent Thanksgiving in Boston; they were anxious to get back to Maine for Sunday," Rideout wrote. "[Blanchard] knew those at the Boston office were fully aware of this." Blanchard was also reportedly anxious to get back to Portland for a family reunion that weekend.

Blanchard continued to check in with the bureau throughout the day. While he was away from the ship, Liscomb relayed the order to C.F. Williams, the Boston agent of the Portland line, to hold off the *Portland*'s departure until 9:00 p.m.

According to several newspaper reports, Williams reported that he relayed the order to Blanchard.

"What did he say?" Liscomb asked.

"He said he should go at seven o'clock," Williams replied.

However, Blanchard's son, who visited with the captain before the ship's departure, told a different story to New England historian Edward Rowe Snow. He said that the company had issued the order for Captain Blanchard to sail.

Retired captain John W. Craig, a former colleague of Blanchard's, told the *Boston Globe* that he could not believe that Blanchard went to sea without orders:

Agent Williams stood on the wharf. He was superior in command as long as that steamer was tied up at her pier in Boston, and if he gave the explicit command that the Portland *should not sail at 7 p.m., I cannot see how Captain Blanchard could have disobeyed.*

Dr. Joshua A. Lewis of the Massachusetts state board of charity and Provincetown selectman Marshall Adams shared a similar opinion, according to the December 6, 1898 edition of the *Bangor Daily Whig and Courier*:

Dr. Lewis and Selectman Adams agree that it is the general opinion among the residents and old mariners on Cape Cod that Captain Blanchard never left without orders, or at least against direct orders from the agent of the company. It is not the custom of captains of vessels to go against the orders of their superiors, especially in a case of this kind, and for that reason they believe that Captain Blanchard, a dead man, has been unjustly condemned for the loss of his ship.

At 6:00 p.m., Blanchard encountered an old friend, C.H. Leighton of Rockland, Maine, on the deck of the *Portland*. The *Boston Globe* described Leighton as "a master mariner," who had retired. Leighton was to be a passenger on the *Portland* but opted out due to concerns over the weather.

"By George, captain, I don't think this a fit night to leave port," Leighton said to Blanchard.

"I don't know about that," Blanchard replied. "We may have a good chance."

Leighton was taking no chances. He went back to his brother's house in nearby Chelsea. Other passengers followed Leighton's notion as the weather outlook worsened. It wasn't just humans who bailed out prior to the ship sailing either—stories abound of a mother cat carrying her kittens off the steamer at the last minute. At the other end of the line, the steamer *Bay State*, scheduled to sail from Portland to Boston, had already canceled its run.

Orleans historian Al Snow, whose father was a longtime friend of Blanchard, wrote of the ship's departure in the November 30, 1961 edition of the *Cape Codder*. Snow noted, "By 5 p.m. the 2,283-ton, 191-foot wooden paddle wheel driven luxury liner was full booked with 108 known passengers. There were sixty-eight in her crew." Over the next two hours, even more people packed themselves on board, according to Snow:

The late-comers knew they'd have to sit up all night for all staterooms had been sold. For the women, stewardesses customarily provided pallets;

mattresses laid upon her carpeted deck, abaft the pilot house. In that cabin space, under blankets, they'd be comfortable. This swelled the total to near two hundred. There was no count.

As the ship prepared for its departure under a full moon, Boston's India Wharf was now shrouded in darkness. High tide was at 10:00 p.m., just in time for the arrival of a developing low-pressure area to the south. The *Portland* departed India Wharf at 7:00 p.m. Snow reportedly began to fall at 7:37 p.m., and two hours later, wind speeds along coastal New England were approaching hurricane force.

As the *Portland* was departing the harbor, Captain Jason Collins of the *Kennebec* is said to have blown his steamship's whistle as a warning to the *Portland* to turn around. There was no response. According to Tom Seymour's summary of the *Portland* disaster in the October 2014 newsletter *Fishermen's Voice: News and Comment for and by the Fishermen of Maine*, "[T]he *Kennebec* had left Boston Harbor ahead of the *Portland*, but taking conditions into account, Captain Collins decided to turn about and return to Boston Harbor."

At 9:00 p.m., Captain William Roix was guiding the steamer *Mount Desert* from Rockland, Maine, to Boston. Roix told an Associated Press reporter that, at this time, he was passing by the Graves, a line of rocky islands along the outskirts of Boston Harbor, and spotted the *Portland*. Roix said that the weather "was very threatening and it was snowing hard." Fifteen minutes later, the storm increased in intensity. The report, published in the December 2, 1898 edition of the *Portland Daily Press*, added:

> *The pilothouse crew on the* Mount Desert *looked astern frequently, fully expecting that the* Portland *would turn around and put back, and did not think it possible that the host would try for Portland. Blanchard must be crazy, Captain Roix remarked to someone in the pilothouse at the time.*

At about 9:30 p.m., Captain William Thomas of the schooner *Maud S.* was returning to Gloucester, fresh off a fishing expedition just northeast of Cape Ann earlier. Thomas and his crew spotted the *Portland*, "with lights burning and paddlewheels churning," according to William U. Swan's summary of the storm for *Cape Cod Magazine* in 1921. The *Portland*, he noted, was on schedule, and conditions were still relatively moderate in the area of Thacher's Island, near Rockport:

Captain Thomas said that he thought the steamer seemed a little nearer shore than usual, in fact she nearly ran him down, so close did she brush by.

Swan speculated that the *Portland* then "won her way across the lower part of the Gulf of Maine until she was near, if not abreast of, Boon Island," perhaps near midnight. However, Deborah Marx of the National Maritime Historical Society thought that any events following the *Portland's* pass of Thacher's Island were questionable:

At this point we can only speculate what happened next. Did the high winds and massive waves overwhelm the vessel? Did a machinery failure cause the ship to lose power, allowing it to swing broadside to the waves?

Captain Ansel Dyer, whose nephew was the quartermaster on the *Portland*, told the *Portland Daily Press* his theory about what happened:

When Captain Blanchard found he was near the shore, he let go both anchors, in my opinion, in an effort to bring her head to the wind but her ground tackle would not hold her. Captain Blanchard was a skillful sailor and a brave man. I knew that he was cool to the last and went down after doing all that he could to save his ship.

The *New York Journal* offered this analysis in its November 30, 1898 edition:

Without casting any reflection on the Portland's *staunchness, seafaring men conjecture that the first effect of the stress of weather was to disable her engines. Thus rendered helpless, they think that she was driven at the mercy of the storm until she fetched up on the boiling Cape Cod shore, with a captain and crew utterly unable to do anything that might stave off destruction.*

Al Snow painted a picture of what may have happened for the Eastham Historical Society:

Portland's *bright deck lights were spotted off Cape Ann, two inbound Boston vessels reported her pitching and rolling, her side wheels out in the increasing storm. Imagine her passengers, tossing/bracing in stateroom bunks, in stateroom areas, where stewardesses arranged for women without staterooms. Imagine engineers and firemen below—performing on slippery decks sloshing in ankle-deep bilge water.*

Four quartermasters were manning the six-foot steering wheel. Unable to shelter around Newburyport, the *Portland* was swept across the bay. Blanchard was hoping to reach Provincetown Harbor, but the winds, switching to the northwest later on, made that task more difficult.

A spare wheel in the *Portland*'s pilothouse offered another possible clue to what happened during the ship's final hours. According to the December 3, 1898 edition of the *Bangor Daily Whig and Courier*, the wheel washed ashore on Nauset Beach in Orleans. The wheel was kept in a cylinder about three feet behind the main wheel, with a steersman between the two:

> *The wheel was lashed with a rope and the knots indicated that only a seaman could have done it. It is thought now that no attempt was made to use this wheel, because the pilothouse was probably washed away the first thing after the steamer's engines broke down, and fell off into the trough of the sea.*

Captain Ansel Dyer told the *Portland Daily Press* that he spent Saturday afternoon on the steamer talking with his nephew, believing "that the weather looked a little dubious but he did not regard it as particularly threatening." He nearly made the trip but had no personal belongings with him. The captain then offered his conclusion as to the ship's fate:

> *It is Captain Dyer's idea that the* Portland *was thrown on her side when far up the coast and the tilt was impossible to bring her head to the wind. Then with one guard pressed down under the water and the other high in the air the ship was driven the forty miles to a point off Highland Light.*

According to the December 1, 1898 edition of the *Boston Globe*, the younger Dyer first entered the employ of the steamer company in 1894 but left to fill a similar position for the Merchants and Miners' transportation company of Baltimore. He came back to the steamer *Portland* in 1897. Dyer was survived by his wife of one month.

The senior Dyer told the *Globe* that, in 1862, he took his then fourteen-year-old nephew on his first long voyage. He followed his uncle to Liverpool and Antwerp before joining the U.S. Navy. "He weighed 210 pounds and could handle himself in almost any kind of a scuttle, but his heart was as big as that of an ox," his uncle said.

H. Arnold Carr, a Massachusetts Division of Marine Fisheries employee who was part of the expedition to locate the *Portland* wreck in 1989, told the *Standard-Times* of New Bedford in 1998 that the vessel was no match for the elements:

> *It was a side-wheeler and it just got overwhelmed. The winds were so severe, they probably lost steering and began taking on water, and then they took a sea broadside. The ship obviously was torn asunder.*

Captain John W. Craig told the *Boston Globe* that turning the *Portland* around was not an option. "When he realized the severity of the storm, and it had gotten by Gloucester Harbor, it was too late to turn back," Craig said, adding that there was likely nothing left of the vulnerable steamer above its hull six hours after passing Thacher's Island. Craig opined that the officers, whose quarters were on the hurricane deck, were the first to perish. He concluded:

> *To my mind, the upper works went over in deep water, and the bodies are pinned in the wreckage, where they will remain until the sea rots the wood and releases them. The hull, after losing the upper works, drifted on for some time.*

While many historians believe that the last time any human being laid eyes on the *Portland* was late Saturday night along the North Shore of Massachusetts, Miriam Bragg of Brewster offered another account to the Brewster Historical Society in 1971. Bragg's father, Captain Allen S. Bragg, and his vessel, the *Mary A. Tyler*, were en route from Maine to New York and found themselves caught up in the storm. The *Mary A. Tyler* eventually wrecked along the Brewster Flats in Cape Cod Bay, and the men were rescued. According to Miriam Bragg:

> [Captain Bragg] *told me too he passed the* Portland, *so close he could have touched it—but he could give no help.*

In his book *New England's Disastrous Weather*, Edward Rowe Snow wrote that the schooner *Grayling* spotted the damaged *Portland* fighting to stay on track at about 11:00 p.m. Within the next hour, the *Florence E. Stream* and the *Edgar Randall* both saw the *Portland*, which had suffered superstructure damage. The *Randall* was reported to have just missed hitting the steamer.

The *Portland* never arrived at its namesake city, taking a turn out to sea. Whether Blanchard headed east to ride out the storm and avoid a possible stranding along the coast, or if the steamer was blown out to sea, has been debated since the disaster.

It was noted in the December 20, 1898 edition of the *Boston Daily Advertiser* by A.B. Johnson of the U.S. Lighthouse Board that many of the lightships broke free and drifted eastward, such as the *Handkerchief Lightship* in Nantucket Sound. Johnson believed that the *Portland* was probably taken in a similar fashion. "If the wind had been stiffer about the time she was off Race Point she would have doubtless made Cape Cod Bay, and not perished off Truro, as was the case," Johnson said.

In his book *Sea Stories of Cape Cod and the Islands*, retired Coast Guard captain Admont Gulick Clark detailed this possible scenario:

> *Those last hours aboard the ship must have been a perfect hell for everyone, especially the passengers with little or no experience of the fearful power of the sea, as the ship's superstructure was stripped off, as the luxurious furniture—chairs, beds, and anything loose careened across their state rooms and the saloon and dining room.*

Early Sunday morning, Captain Sam Fisher of the U.S. Life-Saving Station at Race Point in Provincetown claimed to have heard four whistle blasts, signaling a vessel in distress. He suspected that the blasts were from the *Portland*. Captain Michael Hogan, fighting for the lives of his crewmen aboard the fishing schooner *Ruth M. Martin*, also believed that he spotted the steamer off Provincetown. There was also Lillian Small's account of how she spotted the ship during a brief lull in the storm. Like Bragg's account, whether these sounds and sightings were the *Portland* or not have never been verified.

On Sunday, December 4, 1898, the *Boston Post* published an Associated Press report that "a flask containing a message purporting to have come from Captain Blanchard of the steamer *Portland* was picked up" on Nantasket Beach in Hull, just south of Boston and across the bay from Provincetown:

> *The message reads: "Help! On board the Portland. We are sinking. Upper works gone; two miles off Highland Light. Time, 7:30 Sunday. Blanchard"*
>
> *No credence is placed in the authenticity of the writing.*

While the contents of the bottled message were in doubt, the *Portland*'s final resting place wasn't far from Highland Light. The steamer went down over

Captain Sam Fisher of the U.S. Life-Saving Station at Race Point in Provincetown claimed to have heard four whistle blasts, which he thought may have been the *Portland* in distress. *Author's collection.*

Stellwagen Bank, now a National Marine Sanctuary in Massachusetts Bay, between Cape Ann and Cape Cod. The sanctuary is named for U.S. Navy Commander Henry Stellwagen, who charted the area for the government in 1854. The ship's remains now lie on the sea floor, 460 feet below the surface.

In the days following the sinking, speculation began to build that the *Portland* met its end off the tip of the Cape, striking the dreaded Peaked Hill Bars off Provincetown or just off Highland Light in Truro. Steward Edward Lodge of the fishing schooner *May Gobral*, who was well acquainted with the bay, was more on target. He told the *Boston Post*, "The fishermen of Provincetown were nearly all of the opinion that the *Portland* foundered on the edge of the middle bank, ten miles from the Cape." Captain John W. Craig believed that the *Portland* "finally sank somewhere in the vicinity of Race Point, probably several miles out." Craig added, "Thirty tons of iron was put in her stern. When the hull commenced to sink it went down like a flash."

As debris from the *Portland* began to wash ashore, many speculated that the steamer had collided with another vessel, possibly the *Addie E. Snow* or steamer *Pentagoet*, which both perished nearby.

In mid-December, the *Boston Globe* sent a tugboat to comb the coastline off Provincetown and Truro in an effort to locate the *Portland*. Captain George Eldridge of Chatham—a hydrographer who was on the *George M. Bibb* as "commander's counsel" with Commander Henry Stellwagen while charting

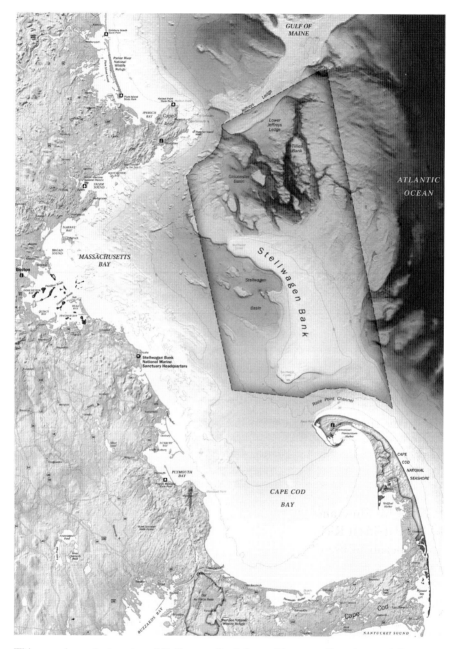

This map shows the location of Stellwagen Bank, located between Cape Ann and Cape Cod. The *Portland* went down on the southern end of the area, which is now a National Marine Sanctuary in Massachusetts Bay. *National Oceanic and Atmospheric Administration.*

the maritime bank named for him—had spent forty years in this profession by the time of the *Portland* Gale. He believed that the steamer was lost just north of Race Point, perhaps on the southern tip of Stellwagen Bank. Eldridge, described as "an eminent authority on tides and currents" by *Cape Cod Magazine*, predicted that "it is possible that the fishermen may at some day not far distant sweep the *Portland* with their trawls."

A few months later, Eldridge's words proved to be correct. In March 1899, relics of the *Portland* were pulled from the surf over Stellwagen Bank in the trawls of the schooner *Maud S.*—the same vessel that spotted the *Portland* off the North Shore of Massachusetts on November 26. The items included a frame from the ladies' cabin, cross pieces and electrical fixtures.

The Stellwagen Bank National Marine Sanctuary in Massachusetts Bay is named for U.S. Navy Commander Henry Stellwagen, who charted the area for the government in 1854. *U.S. Navy.*

The author Edward Rowe Snow spent several years searching for the *Portland* remains but came up empty. Snow met with descendants of those lost on the steamer, hosting an annual memorial ceremony. He also led the efforts to place a commemorative plaque at Highland Light in Truro in 1948.

After searching for several years, the Bourne-based Historical Maritime Group of New England—led by shipwreck hunters John P. Fish and H. Arnold Carr of Bourne and Pete Sachs of Falmouth, along with associates William McElroy and Chip Ryther of Falmouth and Martha's Vineyard summer resident Richard Jones—was able to locate the wreck. In 1986, the group began to use drift analysis to locate the steamer. According to the April 15, 1989 edition of the *Cape Cod Times*, "[D]rift analysis uses sonar systems, precision navigation and extensive computer research to plot the trail of recovered debris and backtrack to possible wreck sites."

The group found a likely wreck in the fall of 1988, but weather conditions forced postponement of further evaluation of the site until April 1989. The *Cape Cod Times* said that the group "made detailed sonar records that clearly showed the upside-down hull of a walking-beam paddle wheel steamer, broken into two pieces." The *Portland* was the only ship of that description sunk in Massachusetts Bay, Fish said. As to whether they thought the steamer was involved in a collision with another vessel, Carr told the *Cape Cod Times*, "We think not. As far as exactly what happened, we really don't know."

In 2002, specialists with the National Oceanic and Atmospheric Administration confirmed the finding. According to the Stellwagen Bank Sanctuary's website:

> Portland *lies upright on a mud bottom with its wooden hull nearly intact from the keel up to the main deck level. The vessel's entire superstructure is missing, with only the steam propulsion machinery protruding above deck level. In addition to the wooden hull and engine, smaller cultural artifacts lie scattered inside and outside the hull, providing a glimpse of the steamer's amenities used by passengers and crew.*

David Faye, a lawyer from Cambridge, Massachusetts, was one of the divers on an expedition in 2008. He told the Associated Press that the ship's wreckage was littered with plates, dishes, mugs, washbasins and toilets, along with a few medicine bottles etched with the name of an apothecary in Maine. The divers found no human remains, believing that they were probably below the decks. Divers didn't explore the interior of the vessel due to the high risk of danger and sanctuary regulations that prohibited exploration of sunken vessels. "I immediately thought of these people—how horrible it must've been," Faye said. "They had no communication with shore. They had no idea where they were. The storm was pushing them out to sea."

Agent C.F. Williams of the Steam Packet Company, critical of Blanchard in the days following the disaster, changed his tune when talking to reporters later that week. The *Portland Daily Press* quoted him in its December 2, 1898 edition:

> *Blanchard was considered one of the most careful men in the company's employ, and we cannot conceive that he would lose his boat without making every effort to save the lives of the passengers.*

A court investigation after the catastrophe released the Portland Steamship Company and Blanchard from any blame. The official finding was that the *Portland* foundered through an act of God, but it wouldn't be long before the Portland Steamship Company was bought out by Eastern Steamship Company, bringing its fifty-seven-year service between Boston and Portland to an end. Steamships were also on the way out as a transportation option on the high seas. The *Boston Post* offered this viewpoint in its November 30, 1898 edition:

> *It cannot be said, however, that this loss is due to negligence. The storm into which the* Portland *sailed was not foreseen at the time of her sailing. The boats of this line, under skillful management, have made their short voyages with a happy exemption from disaster. But it may be said that it is a warning against the policy of using boats of this class, side-wheel steamers, in a traffic which is exposed, even at rare intervals, to such perils of elementary wrath.*

A Similar Story

Nearly a half century earlier, sometime between 1850 and 1855, the steamer *St. Lawrence* was taking the same route, only in the opposite direction. Like the *Portland*, the *St. Lawrence* was caught in a gale shortly after leaving port. Unlike the *Portland*, all but one of the 238 souls on board lived to tell about it.

The *Portland* was likely driven out to sea by fierce winds, leaving it struggling before being overtaken by the waves. In the case of the *St. Lawrence*, it was more by choice that it ended up near Highland Light in Truro.

Roughly four hours after leaving Portland, the *St. Lawrence*, captained by Cyrus Sturdivant, was caught up in heavy snow and high winds as night fell. By morning, the storm intensified, and Sturdivant and his crew "could not discover the points of land we desired," the captain wrote in his 1879 book, *Sketches of the Life and Work of Captain Cyrus Sturdivant*. "The only safe and prudent alternative was for us to change the course of our steamer, and lay her off shore, head to the sea and storm, which was constantly increasing in roughness and fierceness."

By this time, "there was terrible consternation and alarm among some of the passengers," Sturdivant recalled:

> *One of the crewmen was ordered to secure a lifeboat that became loose, and in doing so, his foot slipped, and he fell overboard and was drowned; the sea being so rough and the storm so fierce that no earthly power could save him.*

The situation continued to worsen. The full load of cargo was tossed overboard to lighten the ship's load. The chief engineer told Sturdivant that the main steam pipe might give out and sought instructions on what to do.

"Continue to do your duty as you always have done and we will all do the best we can, and so trust in God who holds the storms in his hands," the captain replied.

The engineer went to the upper deck to attempt a fix. Like many others on board, he dropped to his knees and prayed for help. By evening, "we found ourselves six miles north of the highland of Cape Cod, thankful to God that the gale had become a calm, and so we were saved from finding a watery grave, or being dashed upon the rough shore of the Cape, from whence there would have been no escape," the captain wrote.

The next day, the *St. Lawrence* made its way into Boston Harbor. While there was great relief among those on board that the steamer made it through the storm, Sturdivant was still obligated to break the news of the crewman's death to his family. "He whom they loved so well, and on whom they depended for earthly support, would be seen by them no more until the sea gives up its dead," Sturdivant wrote.

Ghost Stories

The steamer *Portland* was gone. Most of its passengers went down with the ship. Thirty-eight bodies, along with several fragments of the steamer, would wash ashore on the Outer Cape over the following weeks.

Ghostly tales of those lost on the steamer are still told on Cape Cod. In *Cape Cod Pilot*, Jeremiah Digges (also known as Joe Berger) told the story of Captain John Santos of Provincetown and two of his crew from the trawler *Hetty K.*, who were washed overboard and drowned. The bodies of the two sailors washed ashore, but the captain's body was never recovered. His wooden leg later washed ashore, and his wife, Mary, kept it in a cabinet. "She petted it and talked to it," Digges wrote. Exactly one year later, she saw her husband in the room, with no leg. He sat down next to her and said:

> *Barometer's falling, Mary, and the winds no'theast. We're in for thick weather, and I'll want my store leg to keep me steady when she strikes.*

He pinched her on the cheek, and she let out a scream. The next morning, she had a red mark on that same cheek. That night, a storm hit, and she left the leg out by the fireplace. She heard thumping on the floor overnight but stayed in bed. The leg was still next to the fireplace, but it was now wet.

There was heavy rain the night before, so perhaps that was the reason, she thought, but fear soon overcame her. She contacted her doctor, who suggested that she throw the leg, with weights, into the ocean. "I'm a doctor, and I don't listen to stories," he said. "But Mrs. Santos, I put my tongue to that wood. It don't rain salt water."

Robin Smith-Johnson, author of *Cape Cod Curiosities*, grew up in a nineteenth-century house in East Orleans. She wrote that her family always felt the presence of something "more friendly than menacing" in the house. Over a ten-year period, there were several unexplained incidents. In a barn on the property was a loft, with dark stains in the corner. Her father told her that these were bloodstains from corpses that had washed ashore and were piled there after the disaster.

The *Portland* disaster wasn't the only impact left by the storm. The aftermath of the 1898 gale would be felt on Cape Cod for years to come, as the *Provincetown Advocate* noted in its December 6, 1962 edition:

> *The story still moves Lower Cape folks on a gale-ridden night…the image of an old side-wheeler with terrified passengers, plunging in seas that finally smashed her to kindling.*

CARNAGE ON THE CAPE

The debris of a whole hemisphere of industry has been hurled upon the shores in one homogenous mass. Therein lay the secrets of many lives lost, never to be revealed. Many unfinished journeys are here brought to a sudden end by the hand of destiny.
—Sandwich Independent, *December 6, 1898*

During the predawn hours of November 27, 1898, the winds were still howling outside the Race Point Life-Saving Station in Provincetown. The storm had been raging since 10:00 p.m. the previous evening, and it would be nearly another twenty-four hours before letting up.

At 5:45 a.m., Captain Sam Fisher heard the sound of four whistles, a distress signal, from a steamer at sea. Fisher immediately summoned his charges, harnessing the horse and beach apparatus cart, believing that a rescue attempt at sea was imminent. He also telephoned the Peaked Hill Bars Life-Saving Station to be ready as well, but there was no other sign of a ship in distress.

This was a typical professional response for Fisher, who had been Race Point's keeper for ten years. Like many of the outer Cape surfmen, he was well trained in his craft and cheated death at sea on several occasions. During one rescue attempt, he severely injured his back, and a renowned Boston physician told him that he would die in a few years. "I fooled him," Fisher told the *Boston Globe* in 1915. "The physician is dead now, and I'm still here."

Surfman Gideon Bowley of the High Head Life-Saving Station in Truro discovered the first body from the *Portland* on November 28 at 2:20 a.m. *Sturgis Library Archives.*

From one end of the Outer Cape to the other, surfmen continued to patrol the beaches in search of any vessel in distress. There would be many, including the steamer *Portland*. Twenty-four hours and twenty minutes after the celebrated vessel departed India Wharf in Boston, the first piece of evidence emerged that would confirm the fears of many, that the *Portland* was doomed.

At 7:20 p.m., Race Point surfman John J. Johnson was on patrol, venturing into the teeth of the wind, when he came across a life preserver from the *Portland*. Over the next few hours, Johnson and fellow surfman Jim Kelly found several forty-quart creamery cans, doors and other woodwork. At 11:00 p.m., surfman Edwin Tyler of the Race Point Life-Saving Station encountered even more wreckage.

According to J.W. Dalton's *The Life Savers of Cape Cod*, the first body found was at 2:20 a.m. on November 28, when surfman Gideon Bowley of the High Head Life-Saving Station in Truro found the body of one of the *Portland*'s stewards. At the Cahoon's Hollow Life-Saving Station in Wellfleet, the first identified body, George Graham of the *Portland* crew, was recovered. Graham was one of many African Americans working on the *Portland*, as Walter V. Hickey of the National Archives wrote in *Prologue Magazine* in 2006:

> *African Americans served as crew on many of the coastal steamers in the nineteenth century. From the 1900 U.S. census and the 1901 provincial censuses of New Brunswick and Nova Scotia, I learned that several members of the crew, besides Graham, were black, and that many had been born in Canada.*

Over the next few hours, more victims emerged. All told, thirty-eight bodies—some fully clothed, some nude—washed up on Cape Cod's Outer Beach. Many of the bodies found had watches, which had stopped between 9:17 and 10:00—whether that was morning or evening has never been officially determined. All told, "fully three-quarters of the bodies recovered" were at the Orleans, Old Harbor and Chatham Life-Saving Stations, according to the December 10, 1898 edition of the *Falmouth Enterprise*.

Several newspapers picked up the account given by Dr. Maurice Richardson of Beacon Street in Boston, who was at his summer home in Wellfleet during the storm. He saw two bodies wash ashore, both with life preservers from the *Portland*:

> *One was probably a deckhand, a man of about twenty. The other body was that of a stout woman. I picked up three piano keys and a piano cage ashore, but, of course, I do not know they were from the* Portland*. Among the wreckage was in a large quantity of furniture upholstered in red plush. Then there were cases of lard directed to Portland.*

The undertakers' rooms in Provincetown were full. A *Portland Daily Press* reporter took note of one of the victims there. "[She] came ashore with a cruel cut on her head, evidently caused by contact with a piece of wreckage in the water after the steamer broke up," he wrote. "It was believed that was the cause of death." Fred Freitas and Dave Ball must have taken accounts such as this into consideration when they came up with this evaluation in their book *Warnings Ignored!: The Story of the Portland Gale—November 1898*:

> *Those inside were thrown into the icy water as the wooden deckhouse disintegrated, some being killed outright by falling beams and other debris.*

SURFMAN GIDEON BOWLEY FINDING THE FIRST BODY WASHED ASHORE FROM THE WRECKED STEAMER.

This *Boston Post* sketch shows a surfman recovering the body of a *Portland* passenger in the waves. Thirty-eight bodies were found along Cape Cod's outer beach. *Author's collection.*

While Provincetown, Truro and Wellfleet were closer to the scene of the *Portland*'s sinking, many bodies turned up along the shore from Eastham to Monomoy. In Eastham and Orleans, there were more bodies than the local authorities could handle. Rick Lindholm, whose great-grandmother Elizabeth (Brown) Turner was the great-granddaughter of Benjamin Collins, the one-time state senator and keeper at Nauset, passed on the story to him. Lindholm noted that the funeral home on Bridge Road was full, so many of the bodies were kept in a nearby barn. In the *Cape Codder*, Al Snow reported in 1961 that William H. Snow and Gideon Smith pulled the body of a waiter from the *Portland* out of the surf.

Corpses were believed to have drifted even farther south than Monomoy, perhaps vanishing in Nantucket Sound. Remains continued to wash ashore in the early months of 1899, when a body with no hands or feet was found. The *Sandwich Observer* reported in 1911 that a skeleton, believed to have come from the wreck of the *Portland*, was dragged up by a trawl of the schooner *Annie Perry*, ten miles off Chatham. It was dropped back into the sea.

In February 1911, the *Denver Republican* ran a feature story on the perils of the Cape Cod lifesaving surfmen, detailing what can happen to a body in the open sea:

> *The bad seas batter the man overboard severely. Although life preserver enwrapped, he is more often beneath than above the surface, gyrated and tumbled heels overhead by the riotous jumble of driven waters. And if it emerges after only a few minutes of immersion, it is with clothing burdened with many pounds weight of sand—the grains sucked from ocean's floor and held in solution actually being forced through the garment's filaments by the stupendous pressure of which those boiling waters are possessed.*

Steering wheels from the *Portland* turned up in Truro and Orleans. At Highland Light, the four-foot-diameter spoked steering wheel came ashore and was taken home by one of the local surfmen. According to Brad Lynch's article in the September 13, 2002 edition of the *Barnstable Patriot*, Charles Lincoln Ayling—an insurance company executive, collector and benefactor from Centerville—answered a classified advertisement for a clock placed by the surfman. While at his home, he noticed a large object covered in a tarpaulin and was told by the surfman's wife that it was from the *Portland*. "I wish he'd get rid of it," she said. Ayling took it home and donated it to the Centerville Historical Society.

Above: Captain Rufus Snow of Orleans poses next to a steering wheel and other wreckage from the *Portland* that he found on Nauset Beach after the storm. *Eastham Historical Society*.

Left: A pedestal from the *Portland* was recovered by the family of Sheila Mott following the storm, and it has been kept in the family ever since. *Glenn and Sheila Mott*.

A deck stanchion, or spindle, was recovered along Cape Cod's outer beach following the *Portland* disaster. As of 2021, it was on display at the Eastham Historical Society's 1869 Schoolhouse Museum. *Author's collection.*

Captain Rufus Snow, a weekender at the "Sands City" cottage colony along Nauset Beach, found the *Portland*'s big six-foot double steering wheel near his cottage, with two hundred feet of line attached. The *Portland Daily Press* reported that "the wheel was lashed strongly and had evidently been abandoned by the pilots before the ship went to pieces." According to Al Snow, the captain went on an exhibit tour with the wheel to various New England cities, but the Portland Steamship Company had it seized, claiming that "it would ruin their business."

A pedestal from the ship was recovered by the Canham family on the beach in Eastham and, as of 2022, was still in the family's possession. According to owners Glenn and Sheila Mott, "[A] twin of it is pictured in one of Edward Rowe Snow's books." A deck stanchion, or spindle, was recovered along Cape Cod's outer beach following the *Portland* disaster. As of 2021, it was on display at the Eastham Historical Society's 1869 Schoolhouse Museum. Another pole from the *Portland* is displayed at the Dennis Maritime Museum in West Dennis. The *Falmouth Enterprise* reported that stateroom doors from the *Portland* were in abundance, and many were taken by memento seekers on the beach:

> *Most of them have the enamel numbers on, and on many of the doors the lock bolt projected, showing that some of the staterooms had been locked at the time of the disaster.*

Surfman Ben Eldredge of the Old Harbor Life-Saving Station told the *Cape Cod Standard-Times* in 1967 that he was in the station's cupola looking through the spyglass when he spotted "something that appeared to be a log." He took along another surfman, went into the dory and picked up the body of a woman. "All she was wearing were shoes, stocking and garters," he said. Another victim, a fisherman from Maine, "had clothes on complete to comforter wrapped tightly around his head." One victim, a man, "was a discharged Spanish-American war veteran. In his pants was his watch and chain." The Monomoy Life-Saving Station found nine bodies, as did Old Harbor and Orleans. Eldredge said that one pair was identified as a bride and groom.

The storm also cut off most of the Cape's communication and transportation systems to the rest of the world. Telegraph lines were down in many parts of the peninsula. By Monday, November 28, the lines were working only between West Barnstable and Orleans. The following day, the *Sandwich Independent* reported that "large gangs of men are at work in the several localities repairing damage to the road bed and telegraph lines, but the task is an appalling one."

THE RAILROAD

The railroad took a major hit, most notably in North Truro and Sandwich. The *Chatham Monitor* reported that the tracks in Truro experienced "a serious washout" near the station, where the track crossed the Pamet River. A long section of the roadbed approaching the bridge was entirely washed away. The December 6, 1962 edition of the *Provincetown Advocate* recalled a story of how "Boston-bound funeral train" of corpses were able to be transported:

> *Because the railroad trestle in Truro had been weakened by the storm, the coffins had to be conveyed by hand car over the trestle—so the story goes— to another train waiting at Grove's Crossing.*

At Town Neck between Sandwich and Sagamore, three to four miles of track were washed out, as well as three hundred feet of track at the brickyard in West Barnstable. The *Boston Daily Advertiser* reported that "a tidal wave" crossed the railroad track and covered parts of Main Street in Sandwich with three to four feet of water. Several fish houses were wrecked, with one

The railroad in Sandwich sustained heavy damage. This photograph shows the lopsided tracks at Town Neck. *Sandwich Town Archives.*

A toppled fish house sits on the railroad tracks in Sandwich after high tides washed into town from Cape Cod Bay. *Sandwich Town Archives.*

of them being stranded on the railroad track. "The track both east and west of the station uplifted from its bed and laid some fifteen feet away and the embankment or bed was carried off into the marsh." In a letter to the Pratt family, Benjamin Haines wrote that "the track both east and west of the station uplifted from its bed and laid some fifteen feet away and the embankment was carried off into the marsh."

On Sunday, J.N. Smith, a train dispatcher from Hyannis, went up on the train as far as West Barnstable and then walked from there to Buzzards Bay, where he spent the next two days dispatching trains. "He is the right man in the right place," the *Chatham Monitor* said. "Wish we had more like him." The *Yarmouth Register* reported that Fred Hallett of Yarmouth Port was at Sagamore with his horses, transferring people between the trains where the track was washed out.

The first mail to reach Barnstable by train after the storm was received on Tuesday afternoon. A train came through Wellfleet on Tuesday afternoon, but it brought no mail. In Harwich, the Monday morning train over the Chatham branch came up on time and continued to run throughout the day. The *Falmouth Enterprise* reported that a train left Falmouth at 8:27 a.m. on Monday and finally reached Middleboro (where snowdrifts were reported to be ten feet high) at 5:00 p.m. before returning with the morning mail at 9:30 p.m.

THE CAPE'S GATEWAY

Newspaper reports from Provincetown to Plymouth, extending down to Falmouth, Martha's Vineyard and Plymouth, all told of trees being uprooted, house chimneys blown over, buildings unroofed or leveled and boats and vessels in the harbors being driven ashore.

The *Boston Daily Advertiser* reported in its November 30, 1898 edition that the bodies of two young hunters, nineteen-year-old Russel Haskins and twenty-year-old Ernest Raymond, were found by the side of an old wreck on the beach in Plymouth. The paper speculated that "they were probably driven out of their gunning shanty by the sea, and ran to the wreck, hoping to save themselves, and there died, clinging to the old vessel."

Several vessels were reported ashore in Plymouth, including the sloop *Nancy* of Provincetown, sloop *Vesta* of Plymouth and the gasoline launch *Jamaica*, owned and operated by Henry Abbey of Sagamore. The storm also affected the Eel River, which "runs across into the sea instead of out of the harbor," the *Advertiser* reported. One fisherman described the way the cottages on Plymouth Beach were destroyed:

> *The waves first lifted them, and then the gale, getting under them, would carry them up in the air, where they burst in fragments like a shell, scattering contents and timbers far and wide.*

Fred Freitas and Dave Ball compiled several news items for *Warnings Ignored!* The Plymouth waterfront was flooded at high tide on November 27, with the sea completely surrounding Plymouth Rock. The bridge at Town Rock was washed upstream. Only 2 of the 141 cottages along the beach remained standing. The baggage and ticket room at Pilgrim Wharf was wrecked, and the Plymouth Yacht Clubhouse was carried away.

In the Ellisville section of south Plymouth, the high tide "came over the top of the cranberry bog dike, and deposited lobster pots on the area between our house and the barn," wrote Ernest C. Ellis in his book *Reminiscences of Ellisville.* "It would seem that there had been a strong current of tide that had followed up the brook that drains the cranberry bog to Salt Pond, and brought in debris."

Sandwich, the oldest town on Cape Cod, was not only dealing with a flooded railroad track but also so much more, according to the *Advertiser*:

Churches were damaged, houses unroofed, chimneys thrown down and several barns and small buildings were demolished. The streets were impassable from falling trees, which included immense elms and silver oaks, the pride of the town. The loss of livestock was heavy. Many houses were surrounded by the water and some were flooded. One family was rescued in a boat.

The November 29, 1898 edition of the *Sandwich Independent* described the impact of the high tide on the town:

A cyclone…was accompanied by a tidal wave, the like of which was never before seen in this vicinity. Over the marshes came a solid wall of water, some four feet in height. Sweeping over the railroad in several places the water passed the low lands and in two places, below the residences of C.H. Blackwell and B.F. Chamberlain, Main Street, was covered to a depth of three to four feet. For some hours the water remained.

According to an undated newspaper clipping in the Sandwich Town Archives, the Humane House floated to Town Neck from the beach, and many houses had several feet of water on their ground-level floors. The storm also claimed several landmark trees that lined Sandwich's main

On Main Street in Sandwich, "the saddest sight of all was the ruin wrought among the noble shade trees," the *Sandwich Independent* reported. *Sandwich Town Archives.*

streets. Large elms in front of Burbank's and Chipman's Store were leveled. The *Independent* offered this summary of the damage:

> *The saddest sight of all was the ruin wrought among the noble shade trees. Gigantic elms and silver oaks, the pride of Sandwich and the beauty of her streets, were uprooted and prostrated. In front of the M.E. Church, now less than six are gone, with a number of others farther up the street and over the village, the trees suffered a like fate. In many places, the streets were impassable.*

The following spring, the *Sandwich Observer* reported that "the selectmen are having new ornamental trees planted on all the streets, which are very much needed."

The *Independent* noted that the family of James H. Grady was rescued by a boat. Pigpens, stables and henhouses were overflowed, and the loss of livestock was heavy. The roof of the Dan'l Webster Inn was damaged. Haines noted that "the old Boston & Sandwich [Glass] Works were damaged," and "one end of the Cape Cod Glass Works, now Spurr's, is a heap of ruins." More than 150 chimneys were toppled.

Sandwich's churches weren't spared. St. Peter's Church, originally built in 1830 before a larger brick building was constructed in 1854, was so

The Dan'l Webster Inn, *shown at left*, sustained damage to the roof from hurricane-force winds. *Sandwich Town Archives.*

badly damaged that it had to be torn down, according to the September 4, 1986 edition of the *Register*. The church, which had brownstone trim with a 160-foot tower, lost a chimney in the storm. At the First Parish Church, front doors were blown from the hinges, several windows caved in and one side of the belfry was torn away, the *Independent* reported. Benjamin Haines described these two church-related incidents:

> One of the sides of the Unitarian steeple part under the clock was ripped off like so much paper and the Orthodox steeple swayed and shivered like a ship at sea, but survived, in angle not exactly perpendicular. Old Mrs. Chipaul was taken out of the house and taken over to Mrs. Briggs, they being afraid that the steeple would fall upon the house and crush it.

Despite all the damage in Sandwich, there were some who enjoyed the foot of snow that fell. "The sleighing is fine and everyone who owns runners is making the most of it," the *Independent* said. In 1981, historian Ray Barlow noted that the high surf of the bay was most generous, delivering everything from coal and packaged salted cod to live lobsters, clams and kelp, which resulted in an abundance of fertilizer for the town.

In the Buzzards Bay section of Bourne, a windmill was blown down, the roof was blown off an icehouse and a shed was carried into an adjoining field. Out in the bay, the thirty-five-foot cat racer *Flight*, "famous in Beverly Yacht Club regattas," according to the *Barnstable Patriot*, sank on Cleveland Ledge. The tower of the Methodist Church in Cataumet was blown off and replaced in August 1899, the *Sandwich Observer* reported in its August 8, 1899 edition.

The *Observer* also told the Sagamore-based story of B.B. Abbe Jr., Arthur Gibbs and a friend from Boston, who were in Abbe's steam yacht hauling some lobster pots off Ship Pond when the storm hit:

> They made for Plymouth Harbor and anchored, when a shanty adrift bore down on them, and they hastily steamed for the shore opposite knocking some holes in the yacht, but landing in safety.

In Falmouth, the wind and snow created mayhem. The *Falmouth Enterprise* reported that a milk wagon, while coming up Main Street, was blown over, with horse, wagon and driver landing in a snowdrift. The house known as the Vineyard Lodge, the summer retreat for prominent wool businessman Edward N. Fenno, "saw large trees in front snapped off like pipe stems and

The house known as the Vineyard Lodge in Falmouth, shown here a few years after the storm, had several of its trees damaged. *Falmouth Historical Society/Museums on the Green.*

lay in the street." On November 29, 1898, the *Portland Daily Press* reported that the shore in Woods Hole was "strewn with wreckage and pieces of vessels. Fully thirty-five vessels and barges have gone ashore and over eighteen lives have been lost." On the same day, the *Chatham Monitor* said that more than 300 trees were blown down in Woods Hole. At the estate of businessman Joseph S. Fay, more than 150 trees blew down and a large windmill was overturned.

THE MID CAPE

In Barnstable, the region known as "Common Fields" was submerged, while the judge's stand on the Fair Grounds was destroyed. The *Chatham Monitor* reported that several fishing dories, fishing gear and four bodies drifted ashore at Sandy Neck. The *Barnstable Patriot* reported another casualty in that area: "[O]n the back of Sandy Neck is the hull of a wrecked vessel, of from 150 to 200 tons, and a large amount of wreckage, among it a Coaster signal marked, 'Emma, Philadelphia,' from which the vessel is supposed to be the *Emma* of Philadelphia." Three bodies were later discovered nearby, the *Boston Globe* reported on December 1, 1898.

All was not lost in Barnstable, however. According to the January 20, 1983 edition of *The Register*, Charles L. Bassett owned bogs on Sandy Neck in the late 1800s. Records showed that his profit margins were shrinking, but the *Portland* Gale changed it all:

> *In November 1898, the Portland Gale struck Cape Cod and in one of its sideshows flooded many of the Neck bogs. Most of the bog owners decided the bogs were no longer worth the cost of repairing the dikes. And so they were let go to seed. In the eighty-five years since the gale, the marsh has reclaimed all the bogs. The only reminders of the fresh water habitat are the dikes and the barkless, branchless trunks of cedars standing in the marsh.*

Sylvester Baxter also summarized the bog story for *Scribner's Magazine* in 1899:

> *A layer of sand had been distributed evenly upon the marsh, covering it just as bogs have to be covered for the purpose. With Aladdin-like hand Nature had done the cartage overnight that commonly demands much toil, time, and expense.*

The *Yarmouth Register* had another unusual account from Sandy Neck. Buildings from the Barnstable barrier beach drifted across the water to Yarmouth Port and were piled high on the uplands. One of the buildings contained a flock of hens, with the birds making the trip safely.

Just to the south in Hyannis Harbor, tugboat operator Fred Dalzell was having a busy time of it on November 27. Five men from the schooner *Matilda Wood* of Maine were forced to abandon their vessel by jumping onto the breakwater, where Dalzell came to their rescue. Dalzell later towed the schooner *John J. Perry* back to the railroad wharf after the boat parted both chains, struck the breakwater and was drifting out of the harbor. The next day, it was noted by the *Chatham Monitor* that fifty schooners were anchored around the breakwater and rode the storm out safely. The *Independent* reported that Captain Moses Sturges lost his sailboat, *Musquket*. The vessel broke from its anchorage and drifted out to sea. In Hyannis, the spire of the Congregational Church was twisted.

Storm tides struck Yarmouth Port hard, carrying away the Mill Bridge, which connected Yarmouth and Barnstable, along with Long Wharf. The remains of more than twenty-five dories were on the meadows between Long Wharf in Yarmouth and Town Dock in Barnstable. William Baker's house on Mill Lane was completely surrounded by water, with nearly one foot over the lower floor. Just east of Yarmouth Port, the New Boston village in Dennis "was an island," according to the *Register*, with "four feet of water separating the inhabitants of that lonely village from Dennis proper." In East Dennis, the *Sandwich Independent* said that cranberry meadows, dykes and roads were underwater, and an old landmark mill, moved to Dennis from Yarmouth in 1769, was blown down. The *Independent* noted that the town's oldest inhabitant said the tide was the highest the town ever saw.

THE LOWER CAPE

The Exchange Building in Harwich Center had several windows blown out, including a large window in the billiard room. The *Harwich Independent* also reported that a large summer house on its editor's premises "was blown bodily a distance of thirty feet and hopelessly wrecked." In East Harwich, the bulkhead and the approaches to Wading Place Bridge were washed away. Fish houses, boats and debris were scattered and piled up near the bridge. In South Harwich, an old building was demolished, with part of it being swept out to sea.

In Chatham, the *Independent* reported that more than fifty boats in the harbor were sunk or blown ashore and that the beach was badly damaged:

> *The waves running over a breakneck pace, threatening to break down the barriers which protect the mainland from the onslaught. If it finally gives way the damage in this and other storms which will follow will be very heavy and cannot be estimated.*

The *Harwich Independent* added that more than two hundred trees were blown down, and Charles Freeman's house was lifted from its foundation. The spire of the Methodist church, which held the town clock, narrowly escaped falling to the ground. The car house at the Chatham railroad depot was "blown flat." The *Chatham Monitor* reported that a building located on Stage Wharf was blown over into the water, broken in pieces and strewn along Hardings Beach.

Orleans saw plenty of devastation. In South Orleans, the *Monitor* noted that "men who have lived here for sixty or seventy years claim that they have never witnessed such a high tide and heavy sea in Pleasant Bay as prevailed here during the storm." Boathouses were washed away, filling the road with wreckage. The cottage of Louis W. Eldredge "was wrenched from its foundation, blown nearly over." Isaac Chase and his family were forced to leave their house, fearing that it would all be blown down. The porch had already been demolished.

Al Snow listed several material casualties of the storm for the *Cape Codder* in 1961. Fans from William H. Snow's windmill in back of his store wrenched off, smashing against the abutting Board of Trade Building. Beach camps overlooking Nauset Beach were destroyed. In the debris of Camp Cummings, Snow noted that "a smashed commode with porcelain chamber pot made in Trenton, New Jersey, was found on a nearby hill with the old mug and its cover unbroken." Three chimneys toppled from Walter Mayo's house overlooking his duck farm.

The body of Maine's John J. Murphy was found on the beach and taken to the local undertaker. John Kane of Boston was a longtime friend of the deceased. "He knew him and loved him as a brother," the December 4 edition of the *Boston Globe* reported. Murphy called on Kane's Egleston Square house before boarding the *Portland* and told the *Globe* the exchange of that meeting:

> *My folks tried to persuade him not to go by steamer, urging as a reason that he would surely be seasick as the weather was bound to be rough, but he only laughed at this advice and left my house between 3 and 4 o'clock on Saturday afternoon to take the steamer home to Portland.*

The Outer Cape

Al Snow's report extended to Eastham as well. The historian noted that Captain Abelino E. Doane's 1790 barn was badly wrenched but remained standing. His yard was coated with sand blown in two miles from the beach. North Eastham's Robert R. Horton found many life preservers, which he exhibited outside his building known as Excelsior Hall. The *Yarmouth Register* reported that the currying shop owned by Edward Clark was blown down. The turnip crop, which was usually harvested in November, was also affected. John Clark's turnips, which had been removed from the ground only two days earlier, were covered by debris.

Wellfleet, which was still recovering from the Bay View Hotel fire earlier that week, saw substantial storm damage to the wharf area. The road leading to Mercantile Wharf and the bridge to Mayo Beach were washed away. The tar factory, sail loft and several buildings at the beach were moved from their foundations. The *Monitor* also noted that "two tidal waves are said to have followed each other in succession after the flood tide."

In Truro, in addition to the railroad track damage, "great patches of foam flew over the cliffs here, 150 feet above sea level," according to the *Monitor*. Even Highland Light, the Cape's oldest lighthouse site, was not spared.

Highland Light was first established on the cliffs of North Truro in 1797, only to be reconstructed twice, the latest occurring in 1857. Isaac M. "Mort" Small was one of many links in the chain of Smalls who oversaw the light. Mort Small, born in 1845, witnessed his first shipwreck, the *Josephus*, in 1849 at the age of four. Later that year, the youngster met a wandering writer named Henry David Thoreau, who gave him "a full quire of white paper and two lead pencils," according to Small's book *Cape Cod Stories*. Small and his wife, Lillian, were also owners of the nearby Highland Hotel and had a skating rink constructed on the land a few years before the storm. The rink was destroyed by the storm's high winds. Small recalled the damage at his home in the *Falmouth Enterprise* in 1931:

> *The gale that night was so terrific that it blew in every window except those of the kitchen in our house. When the first pane blew in, we tried to stuff the hole with a featherbed, which was handy, but the gale sucked it right out and we never found a trace of it again. Then we began boarding up the windows, and the force of the wind was such that ordinary nails would not hold a minute. It is estimated that the wind blew at the rate of 100 miles an hour that night.*

And then there was Provincetown, which was the center of devastation on the Cape. The *Register* added that two icehouses along Beach Point were blown apart, with fragments reaching the railroad track.

On land, the sea invaded from all angles. According to the *Provincetown Advocate*, the water crossed Commercial Street and ran swiftly back nearly to Bradford Street, "submerging all the low-lying land adjacent and surrounding all houses there." The *Sandwich Independent* noted that a section of Commercial Street near Kelley's Corner was flooded in some places to a depth of five feet. Several women were taken out of houses in boats. In the West End, the water crossed the main street and "formed a lake some three hundred feet wide and half a mile long west of the residence of George W. Ellis," with "the biggest inundation between Lancy's Corner and Pleasant Street." Water in the street was nearly waist deep. Dories were briefly the best way to get around. The paper said that "sidewalks were lifted from the foundations, hens were drowned wholesale, and cellars were flooded."

On Provincetown's back shore near the Peaked Hill Bars Life-Saving Station, much of the *Portland*'s freight load was coming ashore, especially some items that might have been useful to the local undertakers, according to Arthur Wilson Tarbell's 1935 book, *Cape Cod Ahoy!: A Travel Book for the Summer Traveler*:

> *A surfman, coming in from his patrol several nights later, exclaimed to his chief, "Cap'n, some cemetery must have washed open. The beach is covered with coffins." The* Portland, *it seems, had a shipment of caskets aboard. When the storm passed, a local woman carried a baby's coffin home in her arms.*

The purser of the steamer *Longfellow*, identified by the November 30, 1898 edition of the *New York Journal* as "McIntyre," made the trip to Boston following the storm and told this story:

> *Mate Smith and I took a carriage and drove over to a section of the beach where the wreckage was reported to be strewn about. This was between the Peaked Hill Bars and Highland Station. This is about four miles from Provincetown. When we arrived we found the beach covered with all sorts of articles and three bodies. There were life preservers marked "The* Portland*" and boxes of merchandise, cigars, etc., consigned to Portland parties.*

At Race Point in Provincetown, surfmen picked up ice pens, skid boards, sails, hatches and parts of debris marked *F.R. Walker*. Wreckage and cargo from the *Portland* was washing up in abundance. The *Sandwich Independent* reported on December 6, 1898, that "barrels and tubs of lard, casks of varnish, barrels of whiskey, cases of wine, vegetables, all sorts of mahogany can finish, stateroom doors, berth boards, bearing numbers, parts of a piano, light upper works, cases of cigars and tobacco, and about fifty life belts marked 'Steamer *Portland*,'" were strewn along the beach.

One piece from the *Portland* that was recovered on Provincetown's back shore had a new life on the other end of the Cape. The *Falmouth Enterprise* of December 14, 1933, reported that W.A. Burch of North Falmouth had a cane that was fashioned by his brother-in-law. "This particular bit was picked up as a heavy window-shutter," the paper said.

In 1931, the *Provincetown Advocate* noted in its September 10 edition that Rene LeMarre of Detroit found a preserver from the *Portland* and gave it to

Manuel Patrick, the proprietor of the Bradford Inn and Wharf Restaurant. The *Advocate* added:

> *That this life preserver has felt the passing of nearly thirty-three years is seen by its condition. The canvas covering is partially torn away revealing the weather-beaten cork beneath. Only the letters -TLAND are left on the worn canvas that remains, and these letters are dim and barely discernible.*

The *Advocate* recalled a human survival story from the storm in its December 16, 1948 edition. Frank Silva of the Wood End Life-Saving Station found a man, identified as Albert F. Hunter of Salem, crawling up the beach from the surf several days after the storm. Hunter was dory fishing off Minot's Light in Scituate when the storm hit, and despite his best efforts to row back to shore, he was pulled farther out to sea. In the dark, he spotted Wood End Light, made it to shore and crawled to safety on the shore.

The *Portland Daily Press* reported that Provincetown wharves, except for one, were ruined. At Central Wharf in the town's west end, a building containing 155 barrels of flour was flooded. Joseph A. Rich, a fresh fish dealer based in both Provincetown and Boston, maintained his headquarters at Central Wharf. The October 15, 1931 edition of the *Provincetown Advocate*

A damaged Union Wharf in Provincetown, which was built in 1830–31, is seen here across from Paine's Wharf. *From the collections of the Pilgrim Monument & Provincetown Museum.*

Union Wharf in Provincetown is shown here as seen from shore after the storm. *From the collections of the Pilgrim Monument & Provincetown Museum.*

noted that after the storm, Rich's place of business was moved to Railroad Wharf in the east end of town. The *Yarmouth Register* reported that Union Wharf, a longtime business center, was demolished, with the packing shed scattered for several miles along the shore.

Many acknowledged the waterfront devastation as a final death blow to Provincetown's once thriving fishing and whaling industry. According to Leona Rust Egan's *Provincetown as a Stage: Provincetown, The Provincetown Players, and the Discovery of Eugene O'Neill,* fifty-five wharves were servicing vessels during the nineteenth century. Whatever was left on the waterfront after the storm became a base for Provincetown's emerging theater community:

> When the Grand Banks and whaling industries declined, the wharves fell into disrepair and eventually crumbled under winter storms and ice. The ferocious Portland Gale of 1898 exacted a large toll. There was no economic incentive to rebuild.

At Long Point Light, located at the very tip of Provincetown, the light keepers found themselves battling the rising tide. "The whole end of the

Many acknowledged the Provincetown waterfront devastation as a final death blow to Provincetown's once thriving fishing and whaling industry. *Cape Cod National Seashore.*

The storm damage along the waterfront of Provincetown's west end was substantial. *From the collections of the Pilgrim Monument & Provincetown Museum.*

Long Point Light, located at the very tip of Provincetown, was underwater during the storm. Floodwaters were four feet deep around the light keeper's house. *Author's collection.*

point was flooded," light keeper Samuel Soper Smith told the *Boston Globe* in March 1899. "It looked as if we would be swept away."

The Smiths were responsible for keeping the fog bell operational, which meant venturing outside to wind it. The light keeper, battling illness, managed to accomplish this, but as he returned to the house, the tide kept rising. "It was four feet deep all around the house," he said. The light's water tank, weighing a ton when full, was lifted by the surging seas and carried out into the bay.

Provincetown was where many thought the *Portland* lurked in the hours following its disappearance. On Monday morning, the U.S. revenue cutter *Woodbury* was sent to search for the missing steamer. The *Woodbury's* first stop was Gloucester, which proved fruitless. "The *Portland* will be found down Provincetown way, or she won't be found at all," the captain told the *Portland Daily Press*. "I am afraid that she is lost."

On the way to Provincetown, wreckage from the *Portland* was seen floating in the bay. The captain then spotted the cutter *Dallas* and reached for a megaphone: "Have you heard anything from the steamer *Portland?*" The answer: "All hands lost."

The *Woodbury* soon anchored at one of the remaining docks in Provincetown. In broken English, Portuguese fisherman began to tell him of the *Portland's* fate. But so much more had happened. "They told the captain other things," the *Press* reported, "which almost made the blood run cold."

Provincetown in Peril

Men who had vessels which were expected to be unfit for further use, as they were being driven ashore, were crying; women who had relatives out at sea were weeping, and children were crying for fear of being washed away.
—Annie Newcomb Spaulding of Greenwood, Massachusetts,
from a composition written for her English class at age fifteen shortly after the
storm, published in the Provincetown Advocate, *December 1, 1938*

Provincetown Harbor has long been considered one of the safest havens for seafaring vessels in New England, so when the storm began raging on the night of Saturday, November 26, mariners from miles around were heading for its cozy confines.

However, the following morning, even Provincetown Harbor was not a safe place. Between twenty-five and thirty vessels took refuge there. According to the U.S. Life-Saving Service, "some foundered at their anchors, some drifted into shoal water and pounded on the bottom until water-logged, and others were driven high and dry on the land." One of the fishing boats was found one hundred feet from the high-water mark.

Many of those on board the stranded vessels survived the ordeal, except for six unfortunate souls aboard the Maine schooners *Lester A. Lewis* and *Jordan L. Mott*. Five were aboard the *Lewis*, representing the full crew, with the other being the *Mott* captain's father. The two vessels were among many that piled up in the west end of the harbor, the general area of where the *Mayflower* had anchored 278 years earlier. A breakwater was constructed

Veteran keeper Isaac "Ike" Fisher, *center front*, led his Wood End crew through high winds and surf for ten hours to rescue shipwrecked men in Provincetown Harbor. *Author's collection.*

here in 1911, 13 years after the storm, so the vessels breaking away from their moorings were buffeted and pounded over several sand bars before being swept high and dry on the west end of the harbor.

At 5:00 a.m., patrolman Frank C. Wages of the Wood End Life-Saving Station was near Long Point, one and a half miles to the east. Through the elemental fury, he spotted what seemed to be a vessel driving ashore. With the furious wind at his back, Wages was able to sprint back to the station. Sixty-one-year-old Keeper Isaac Green "Ike" Fisher, who happened to be in the observation tower, knew that there was trouble. The crew was just rising for the day, but breakfast would have to wait.

The boat was on the inside beach of the thin strip extending out toward Long Point, but pulling the surfboat wagon through the sand and snow was another matter. The hurricane-force winds would likely blow the wagon over, shattering the boat. This forced the crew to push it along, often wading in knee-deep or even chest-deep water. "The gale frequently lifted it up, so that the men had to press it down by main force, and in this way, among dangerous drift logs and wreckage, they pushed on for hours," the Life-

Wood End Life-Saving Station and Wood End Light in Provincetown overlook both the Atlantic Ocean and Provincetown Harbor. *Cape Cod National Seashore.*

Saving Service reported. As John Bell noted in his 1971 account of the storm for the *Provincetown Advocate*, the harbor was packed with wreckage. The crew dragged their boat eastward over this wreckage, finally reaching the mouth of Lobster Plain, a tidal inlet. The wind prevented them from rowing across the fifty-foot channel. One man waded across in icy water up to his neck to bury their anchor in the opposite bank. They hauled the boat across by its painter.

Finally, two sunken schooners were spotted. Utilizing a rope attached to a fish weir, they began to move the boat out in the water, but to no avail, as the Life-Saving Service noted:

> *It was the hardest battle they ever had. There was sore disappointment in their hearts, but they went about their new task with undaunted spirit and much haste as they could, but the sea and drift stuff often took them nearly off their feet, and progress was therefore slow.*

At this point, it was midday, and one man was sent back to the station to get some much-needed food. By 4:00 p.m., they were finally ready to push out, with the wind still forcing them back. With the assistance of four fishermen from the *Mary Cabral*, they double manned the oars, and after two more attempts, they made it off shore.

The first vessel spotted was the *Jordan L. Mott*, sunk to the anchors, with only the cabin and masts above water. "Four men, with benumbed and stiffened limbs, crept down from the rigging as the boat approached, and then when it was pulled close were taken off by the surfmen," the Life-Saving Service noted. The captain's father, who had died earlier, was lashed to the rigging.

All hands had been in shrouds for fifteen hours and were nearly collapsing. According to John Bell's 1971 account in the *Provincetown Advocate*, "Captain Charles Dyer and the ship's boy were nearly dead; their companions had been beating them to keep them from freezing."

The boat was then pulled to the beach in a favorable direction with the wind and landed at about 5:00 p.m. There was a half-hour walk to the station, with the captain and another man being carried due to their condition. They were cared for at the station. It was a full day before the captain could walk again.

Captain Dyer told a reporter later that he had not expected any help from Wood End Station because he could not believe "that mortal man could get a boat up from that direction across such a sea in a hurricane. Fisher and his crew did all they could, more than I thought humanly possible."

A man shows two children the devastation of the schooner *Lester A. Lewis* in Provincetown a few days after the storm. *Cape Cod Maritime Museum.*

"If we had a couple of horses, I believe we could have saved every man on the *Lewis* and the *Mott*," was how Fisher summed up the situation.

The *Lewis* was a hopeless situation. Wood End light keeper Douglas Shepherd recalled in 1928 that the men lashed to the rigging were "garbed in a ghastly shroud of white, and upon a thorough investigation it was seen they were beyond human aid." One frozen corpse was found inside the cabin.

The impact of the horrific story of the *Mott* and *Lewis* was still felt for years. In 1969, the *Provincetown Advocate* recalled a story told by Aaron Shaw about a woman described as "Mrs. Henry Spears," who lived in the West End:

> *Among the Provincetowners drawn by the universal urge to view the scene of death, she watched from her windows while men cut frozen bodies out of the rigging. From that time on, she kept the shades drawn on every window facing the harbor.*

For Ike Fisher, it was another noteworthy accomplishment toward the end of a long and distinguished career. After many years at Peaked Hill Bars Life-Saving Station, Fisher was transferred, with much fanfare from the Massachusetts state legislature, to Wood End Life-Saving Station, where he was allowed to pick his own surfmen, in 1896.

He eventually retired in May 1901 after several weeks of being unable to fulfill his duties as keeper and died in September that year. As Keeper William Cook of the Peaked Hill Bars Life-Saving Station told writer Mary Heaton Vorse many years later, "They don't make cap'ns like him any more."

Harbor Rescues and Wrecks

Many civilians stepped forward to help out in the rescue efforts. Among them were Captain Robert Lavender and a crew of seafaring veterans from Provincetown, who were all awarded the Congressional Medal for Bravery after the rescue of William Forrest from the rigging of the fishing schooner *F.H. Smith* in the harbor during the height of the storm. Each medal was inscribed:

> *In Testimony of Heroic Deeds in Saving Life from the Perils of the Sea, for brave assistance in rescuing a man from the wreck of the schooner* F.H. Smith, *November 27, 1898.*

News of the *F.H. Smith*'s plight reached the fifty-two-year-old Lavender, who had retired from whaling ten years earlier. As the September 12, 1929 edition of the *Provincetown Advocate* put it, "The Call of the Sea seeped through this man's veins." According to *Biographical Sketches of Representative Citizens of the Commonwealth of Massachusetts*, Lavender began going to sea as a young boy and was the master of a fishing vessel at sixteen. He was presented with a silver medal by the Canadian government for his part in the rescue of the shipwrecked crew from the bark *Chili* of Yarmouth, Nova Scotia, in 1878.

Moving into a crowd of local residents, Lavender made his intentions known: "Men, we know that there is one of us out there in the riggin'—it's a life, mates, and I am going to try to get at him. I call for volunteers."

Charles Foster, Everett Horton, Joseph Settes, Captain Ben Bensen, James M. Burke, Joseph Brown, James Lopes, Tony King, James Worth and Charles Forrest stepped forward, but the next concern was obtaining a boat. Burke suggested a seine that he spotted at Tarrant's seine repair shop. Lavender and company proceeded to dig the boat out of the drifting snow. It had some holes and leaked, so the crew brought along buckets for bailing. Down to the water's edge they went, where they were greeted by snow and sleet driven by hurricane-force winds. "This is no ordinary gale," Lavender warned.

Lavender was at the steering oar, with a few members in the middle to handle bailing. As they made it out into the harbor, "a snarling green sea foaming at its crest broke over the stern quarter," according to the *Advocate*. "The monster wave had caught [Lavender] unaware, tore the steering oar from his grasp and knocked him overboard." The December 6, 1898 edition of the *Sandwich Independent* reported that "the steering oar struck Captain Lavender a heavy blow on the head, knocking him ten feet into the icy waters."

Lavender's head quickly appeared above the surface. Shaking his head, he said, "Don't mind me, boys. Keep 'er goin'. I'll make shore all right."

"Like the Devil you will," one of his crewmen replied.

They managed to pull him back on board, to cheers from those watching from the shore. Despite waves breaking over them, they spotted the *F.H. Smith*, with William Forrest still in the rigging. He kept from freezing by keeping constantly in motion, ascending and descending the rigging.

The masts were about to topple as Lavender and his crew approached the *Smith*. "All right, Matey, you swing clear of the shrouds and gear and let go," Lavender yelled to Forrest. "We'll take care of you." He dropped into the sea but was quickly pulled into the rescue boat. The *Advocate* marveled at the volunteers' efforts:

It was utterly beyond human strength to pull back from whence they started.
Some three hours later these brave, hardy men of the sea landed on the west
shore of the harbor, where willing hands hustled them to their homes, where
they rested after their heroic labors.

They next visited the *Frank Foster*, which had been torn to shreds during the night, but found no men. It wasn't long before the wind carried the vessel out of sight.

The Gloucester fishing schooner *Carrie Hayward*, a fifty-five-ton craft under the command of Captain Charles Horne, went ashore along the harbor after riding out the storm on the night of November 26. Fisherman John Daniels, described by the November 30, 1898 edition of the *New York Journal* as "a weather-beaten old salt," told the paper of their adventure:

It was the stiffest old blow I ever saw. The wind was blowing so hard that
I couldn't keep my feet on the deck. Sunday morning about 8 o'clock the
captain gave orders to head the craft for the beach—almost into the woods.
The captain and all of the crew of eleven were safe. The schooner was not
damaged a bit but I don't believe they'll take her off now until spring. I
don't want to see another storm like that again, now, I can tell you.

Captain Simeon Studley of Dennisport and the schooner *W.H. Oler* conquered the elements. The June 19, 1941 edition of the *Yarmouth Register* reported that Studley "survived the terror of the Portland Gale when his ship barely made Provincetown Harbor in the rising gale only to escape wreck within the haven when her anchors dragged." The December 5, 1898 edition of the *Barnstable Patriot* put it this way: "The *Oler*…about whom grave fears were entertained about their safety in the recent terrible storm, rode out the gale safely in Provincetown Harbor, having got in just in time." Studley would later spend thirty-two years aboard the lightships around the Cape. He may have survived the deadliest maritime weather event in New England history, but he met his end in June 1941, when he died in an automobile accident in Abington, Massachusetts. He was seventy.

The *Mary Cabral*, which assisted the Wood End lifesavers in the *Mott* rescue, was among the vessels piled on the beach near Wood End, along with the *Sylvester Whalen*, *Philominia Manta*, *A.B. Nickerson*, *Ellen Jones* and *Daniel Boone*. The *Advocate* described the plight of the *Isaac Collins* crew, who were "perceiving that a stranding was inevitable, slipped the cable, hoisted the jumbo and drove westward hard and fast upon the sands." The *Collins* also "completed the task of discomfiting the little craft [*School Girl*] by running into and sinking her off hand while scudding."

Joseph Silva's fishing boat *Nautilus* managed to return from a fishing trip to Block Island at ten o'clock Saturday night, but the confines of the harbor weren't enough to save it from colliding with and driving through Steamboat Wharf, destroying the wharf's bridge. Steamer *Vigilant* was lost after drifting against another pier. The fishing boats *Agnes*, *Champion*, *Ella Francis*, *Inez Hatch*, *Sylvia*, *Lida* and nearly thirty other fine "doggers" were sunk or vanished. The *Success* was riding at moorings, dismasted by collision with dragging schooners.

The fishing schooner *Unique* of Boston, anchored off back of Long Point, was forced to cut away its masts to prevent dragging to leeward. Steamer *Longfellow* brought it into the harbor two days later, then on to Boston. The Wood End Life-Saving crew found the dismasted hulk of the empty schooner *Gracie* of Maine, which was believed to have a crew of five men.

At Race Point, wreckage of the *Portland* came ashore, along with the remains of two other vessels, the *F.R. Walker* and the *Addie E. Snow*. While the consensus is that the *Portland* was overwhelmed by the high seas, there have been many who believed that the steamer collided with another vessel. Some believed that boat was the *Addie E. Snow* of Maine.

According to Mary Melton's 1998 book, *Lost with All Hands: A Family Forever Changed*, the *Addie E. Snow* left Portland on November 26, carrying a load of granite paving stones.

Following the storm, news about the fate of the *Portland* and other ships began to trickle in to the families of the *Addie E. Snow*'s crew. One newspaper report misidentified one of the beached vessels as the *Addie E. Snow*, giving the family false hope. Eventually, the family learned that remains of the schooner washed up at Race Point, and the Mainers ventured to the tip of the Cape to verify what washed ashore. Upon their arrival at Race Point, the family was greeted by light keeper Charles Havender, whose house was described as "damaged living quarters, windows broken by the gale." Havender produced a medicine cabinet with the letters spelling "*Addie E. Snow*."

WRECK OF THE *ALBERT L. BUTLER*

On Provincetown's back shore, the 344-ton schooner *Albert L. Butler* ran aground near the Peaked Hill Bars Life-Saving Station at around 10:00 a.m.

on Sunday. Two of the crew and a passenger were lost. According to the U.S. Lifesaving Service:

> *The sailors perished as a result of their own rashness and lack of self possession, when they might have certainly have been saved. The passenger, from Jamaica, fell from the rigging while the schooner was plunging shoreward, and was beyond any help either from the vessel or the land.*

The *Albert L. Butler*, with a crew of seven, was heading from Jamaica to Boston with a full cargo of logwood. Already having encountered rough seas, the storm intensified as the vessel was forty miles off Highland Light in Truro. After more progress to the north, the ship was driven by northeast gales toward shore. Captain Frank Leland figured that his ship "made a dead drift of about fifteen miles."

By seven o'clock the next morning, the ship was approaching Peaked Hill Bars, considered to be one of the deadliest stretches along the Atlantic coast. According to Robert J. Wolfe's report "Dwelling in the Dunes: Traditional

The 344-ton schooner *Albert L. Butler* ran aground on Provincetown's back shore during the height of the storm. *From the collections of the Pilgrim Monument & Provincetown Museum.*

Use of the Dune Shacks of the Peaked Hill Bars Historic District, Cape Cod" for the National Park Service, the Peaked Hill Bars are named for "several shallow sand bars evidently named for a prominent dune once visible to mariners from the sea." In *Life Savers of Cape Cod*, J.W. Dalton referred to Peaked Hill Bars as "an Ocean Graveyard…a more bleak or dangerous stretch of coast can hardly be found in the United States." Peaked Hill's "victims have been many, and its shouting waters almost seem to voicing the message: 'All hope abandon, ye that enter here,'" the *Denver Republican* said of it in 1911. Two bars, one about 600 yards offshore and the other about 1,400, created the deadly predicament. The *Republican* described the unpredictable surf:

> *Rising as they do from a considerable depth to within a few feet of the sea's surface, their interposition occasions a disruption of the onswinging columns of water that results in a veritable maelstrom over all of the shoal.*

Leland described the sea as "frightful, the biggest I ever saw, and the gale swept us at its mercy." The vessel drifted for three hours until about 10:00 a.m., when "the shore breakers were under her forefoot, and she swung broadside high onto the beach." Surfman Bert Bangs described the *Albert L. Butler*'s impact to Bossy McGady of the *Provincetown Advocate*, as published in 1951. The *Butler* came high over the outer bar, with the Jamaican man clinging to her rigging. When the ship hit the bar, he was "shot into the air like a gull's feather and lost in the surf," never to be seen again.

While on patrol, Peaked Hill surfman B.F. Henderson and High Head surfman Benjamin Kelley spotted the *Albert L. Butler* when it struck the sandbar. The pair was outside the halfway house, the midway point between their stations, but were unable to go inside because of high surf breaking over the hut. They quickly relayed the information to the Peaked Hill Station. McGady wrote that the *Albert L. Butler* "struck on the spot where some 122 years previously the 'Big MO' of her day, the *Somerset*, had come ashore."

The Peaked Hill Bars Life-Saving Station was under the command of Keeper William Cook, who took over for Isaac Fisher in 1896. Cook was born in Provincetown and, at a young age, joined up with the merchant service and then the local whaling fleet, where he became a master with the boat oars. In the Life-Saving Service, he used a twenty-one-foot steering oar, which led to great success in rescues (twenty-six people between 1896 and 1902). In his lectures about the Life-Saving Service, renowned Arctic

The crew of the Peaked Hill Life-Saving Station was quickly on the scene for a rescue attempt of the shipwrecked *Albert L. Butler. Sturgis Library Archives.*

explorer Admiral Donald MacMillan of Provincetown recalled how highly regarded the Peaked Hill keeper was:

> *How we worshipped "Wall" Cook, a hero to every small boy in town. We knew that he was thoroughly acquainted with the sea, that he knew just what tumbling waves would do, for he had followed the sea all his life.*

The Life-Saving Service noted that shortly after 11:00 a.m., the apparatus was set up and ready to go. Keeper Cook fired two shots from the Lyle gun from a high bank, and a sailor on board the *Butler* began to fasten the whip line. However, he failed to do so efficiently, and the man ended up being dragged through the breakers to shore. Shortly after, the mizzenmast gave way and crashed, fouling the rigging and whip line. Two men panicked and, despite warnings from the surfmen, tried to go in as the man before them did. Cook reported:

> *A big sea, I should say twenty feet high, rolled in and buried the vessel, men and everything. I had hold of the whip line, and could feel when the sailors lost their grasp. They were washed off, and that was the last we knew of them.*

Leland washed ashore on a piece of wreckage. He and two other men were pulled up while trying to climb the bank. Leland told the Life-Saving Service:

> *If they* [the lost men] *had worked the lifesaving lines properly, they would doubtless have been saved. They were all used up and badly scared, hardly in a condition to do things in an orderly and sensible way.*

Later on, Cook was told by the surviving sailors that there was no one left on board, but at 2:00 p.m., they spotted smoke from the *Albert L. Butler* cabin's chimney. As the tide was receding, two men, one with a parrot perched on his shoulder, jumped ashore from the schooner. They had retreated to the cabin when the craft struck and stayed in there without the knowledge of their mates. McGady said that Bangs called the parrot "belligerent" and "furious," while uttering some rather salty language. "But if it was referring to the weather," the surfman said, "then I agree with that bird. The 'November gale' was a humdinger!"

HEROES OF THE STORM

It was a night to try men's souls. It was a night when the strongest of men trembled and when women wept. It was a night that should witness deeds of human bravery. It was night of agony and of death.
It was a night when the coast guardsman was remembered.
—Boston Post, *December 4, 1898*

In 1898, the U.S. Life-Saving Service was operating twelve stations along Cape Cod's outer beach. In these outposts between Wood End in Provincetown and Monomoy, just south of Chatham, the "Wardens of Cape Cod," as writer Henry Beston called them many years later, were on alert, watching the high seas for any mariner who might be in distress while battling the Atlantic's elemental fury. The *Boston Post* had high praise for the surfmen:

> *The stations are located away from the habitations of man, and if there be any near, the villagers are asleep and know not of the fearful tragedy that is being enacted on the shore. The crew are face to face with possible, and often probable, death, but there is no wavering. The raging wind howls defiance at them, laughs when the boat touches the water, invites them to combat, gloating almost in victory. And when the fierce fight begins there is no cheer from the shore, only the bleak cliffs hurling back the voice of the storm.*

"Heroes of the Storm" was the headline in the *Boston Post* on December 4, noting that it took a disaster such as this for the public to notice what these

The surfboat was one of the U.S. Life-Saving Service's many tools of the trade when it came to rescuing those involved in shipwrecks. *Sturgis Library Archives.*

men of the U.S. Life-Saving Service faced on a regular basis. The Life-Saving Service, established in 1872, had twelve outposts on Cape Cod's outer beach from Wood End in Provincetown to Monomoy, south of Chatham. The agency became part of the Coast Guard in 1915.

The surfmen were not highly paid, yet their lives were on the line when they launched a surfboat into pounding waves or patroled a narrow beach under towering sand cliffs with a raging tide beckoning.

And yet, there were doubters about their dedication. During the week following the storm, as the surfmen were finding one corpse after another and the constant drum of death continued to beat, battle fatigue began to set in. A daily newspaper had accused them of looting the dead bodies on the beach.

The *Boston Globe* opined that "man of such noble impulses rarely stoop to such base practices as intimated in the article referred to." An unidentified surfman from the Orleans Life-Saving Station told the *Globe* that "only those who do not know us would say such things," noting that many of the bodies had little or no clothing. Whatever valuables found were turned over to the authorities.

While some bodies were found in the surf and others on the sand, some were half buried. "It was a terrible week that we spent," Old Harbor Life-Saving Station surfman Ben Eldredge told Edward Rowe Snow. "Sometimes we could see just a hand sticking up in the sand, and when we dug, of course, we exposed a body."

Isaac M. Small, author of *Shipwrecks on Cape Cod*, wrote of the effect that these regular encounters with death had on the surfmen:

> *Several of them were completely unnerved by their frequent trying experiences in dragging torn and sea-washed bodies from the surf. There were cases where some of the men of this service were made almost nervous wrecks by their almost nightly contact with the disfigured and unfortunate victims thrown up to their feet by the sea.*

The lifesavers were responsible for transporting bodies to the local undertakers for burial. One of the Peaked Hill Bars Life-Saving Station surfmen told a journalist about the transport methods and the gruesome details of some of his encounters. The writer then asked if it was hard on the nerves. According to the Cape Cod National Seashore's "Historic Furnishings Report: Old Harbor Life-Saving Station," the surfman replied, "We can't think about that; you know they are someone's friends."

When a stranded vessel was spotted offshore, the patrolman would light a Coston flare, alerting the men on board that help was on the way and providing a distress signal to his mates at the station. This was usually the beginning of the rescue mission, as longtime Coast Guard surfman Yngve Rongner told the Eastham Historical Society in a 1968 interview:

> *At times a ship might be too near to the surf or in other danger, and a red Coston signal was burned to warn it of peril.*

If surf conditions permitted, a surfboat was launched with several surfmen on board. If the surf was deemed to be too rough, the lifesavers utilized the breeches buoy, a mortar with a projectile attached to a rope that got shot into the rigging of a sinking ship. The top was a lead-line that pulled a heavier rope, the pulley and the lifesaver ring all out to the ship. Once the lines were secured, the survivors could step into the legs of the breeches within the ring and be hauled ashore.

Some of these men were longtime veterans, putting in twenty or thirty years on the job; others were relatively new to the profession. Their compensation was roughly forty dollars per month.

Regarding the severe conditions during the *Portland* Gale, the Life-Saving Service described what the Peaked Hill crew went through while launching

The surfmen of the U.S. Life-Saving Service were often at the mercy of the elements while on patrol. *Author's collection.*

their apparatus cart in the rescue of the *Albert L. Butler* on Provincetown's back shore:

> *It is difficult to convey to a person unfamiliar with the region an intelligent idea of the toil and struggle necessary to drag any sort of loaded vehicle, even a comparatively light one, through the deep and yielding sand. The flying particles at times almost blinded the men and the horse, and now and then they were obliged from sheer exhaustion to halt to regain their breath. To force a way through the deep sand drifts, which they frequently encountered, the men were constantly heaving at the wheels, and the panting horse was compelled to pull and tug with desperate efforts.*

"The wintry wind, laden with sea damps and cutting sands, buffets him sorely as, its shoulders bowed, he combats the gusts that seem aiming to prevent his progress," was the description provided by the *Denver Republican* in 1911. Following the 1895 wreck of the *Job H. Jackson*, the *Barnstable Patriot* described "from mustaches and beards hung great globules of congealed water, the frozen breath of working men."

While the gales and frozen precipitation of a northeaster were bad enough, the surfmen's worst enemy was "the sand." As Arthur Wilson Tarbell wrote in his 1935 book, *Cape Cod Ahoy!*, "Eyes are filled in ordinary blows, but when a 'snorter' rages the face is often cut until the blood comes." The Life-Saving Service reported that the Provincetown rescuers had to "thwart a wind that swept sharp, fine sand through the air in smothering streaks that cut like the strokes of a whiplash."

In her book *Time and the Town*, Mary Heaton Vorse wrote that "in some winds the beach lifts itself bodily. The sand grinds the skin off a man's face. There are patrols that have to be made on hands and knees." Such was the case of Bert Bangs of the High Head station in North Truro at the beginning of the storm. Bossy McGady, in a 1971 column for the *Provincetown Advocate*, told the story of how Bangs crawled on his hands and knees along the ridge of the dunes, with the sea breaking over him. "Several of his fingers were frozen, his face bloody and raw from the driving sand," McGady wrote.

At the Brant Rock Life-Saving Station in Marshfield, surfmen were facing more than sand particles flying through the air shortly before the wreck of the schooner *Mertis H. Perry*, owned by Frank Perry of Brewster. The Life-Saving Service report told of how "the cottages near the shore were toppling over and being swept hither and thither, and their fragments were flying through the air."

Surfmen from the Monomoy Life-Saving Station had issues with the visibility on the beach. Osborne Chase, who had the eight o'clock to midnight shift on the night of November 26, never made it to the halfway house. It was well after daylight when he finally returned to the station after "he got lost—lost all sense of direction and wandered around the beach all night," wrote Clarkson P. Bearse in his book *The Tragedy of Monomoy Beach*.

Seth Ellis of Harwich, covering the midnight to 4:00 a.m. shift, was the next Monomoy patrolman to head out on the partially flooded beach. In 1902, he was the only surviving surfman from the attempted rescue of the crew from the barge *Wadena* and was later promoted to keeper. Ellis was the only surfman to reach Point Rip at the tip of Monomoy on the night of the *Portland* Gale. Guided by the volume of the roaring surf, he kept to the center of the beach. The high-water mark of the beach was marked by weir poles, which aided Ellis when he reached the halfway house, although it was a challenge for him as well, Bearse noted:

> *Unless you have been there you cannot imagine the tremendous sickening roar of the surf combined with the shrieking of the wind in a storm like the Portland Blizzard.*

On Martha's Vineyard, the men of the Gay Head Life-Saving Station were on duty from 11:00 p.m. on November 26 until the late afternoon of November 28, much of it dealing with the rescue of the schooner *Amelia G. Ireland*. "Several had received painful injuries," wrote Sylvester Baxter in *Scribner's Magazine*. "Of such are the humble heroes to whom fame comes not."

"These men worked like fiends," was how the *Portland Daily Press* described the Provincetown surfmen's efforts. The *Boston Post* told how a surfman, identified only as "Jim," was unable to save three men from a wrecked craft. "I wished I could have saved those fellows," he lamented, but the *Post* offered consolation to the surfman in the feature's conclusion:

> *It's all right, Jim, and you other men of the lifesaving crews. Nigh three hundred souls were lost on that awful night, but you did your best. You are the heroes of the blizzard. Some of you toiled all night alone; some of you walked up and down the wreck-strewn beaches; some manned the boats; some succored the saved at the station houses; all are heroes.*

LOST AT SEA

*The worst is expected. No news. For how many weeks do you suppose the family
and friends of Captain Garfield kept alive a little hope?
Through Christmas perhaps? Or over the New Year celebration?
—newsletter of the Dennis Historical Society, Dennis, Massachusetts,
December 1987*

On the night of November 22, 1898, Captain John D. Garfield of West Dennis and Captain Mark Holmes of New Haven, Connecticut, were dining together in Philadelphia. Over the years, the two had become fast friends through their sailing circles, and both were about to embark on yet another coal run to New England ports. Some ninety-six hours later, the two mariners were together once again, only not in a manner that they expected. Both were lashed to the masts of their respective ships, dead, at the bottom of the ocean off Montauk Point, New York.

Garfield, thirty-six, was the captain of the three-masted schooner *James B. Pace* and a member of the prestigious Boston Marine Society. Holmes was the master of the schooner *Howard M. Hanscom*. On the morning of November 24, both vessels were being loaded with coal—1,200 tons aboard the *Pace* and 1,100 tons on the *Hanscom*. Garfield and the *Pace* were bound for Boston, Holmes and the *Hanscom* for Providence, Rhode Island.

As Lee Gruzen speculated in the November 26, 1998 edition of the *East Hampton Star* of Long Island, "It was likely the two ships had departed from Philadelphia and were sailing together, as coal schooners often did."

Right: Captain John D. Garfield, of West Dennis, and the three-masted schooner *James B. Pace* were lost at sea off Montauk Point, New York. *West Dennis Graded School and Dennis Historical Society Maritime Museum.*

Below: The three-masted schooner *James B. Pace* of West Dennis was lost off Long Island, New York. *West Dennis Graded School and Dennis Historical Society Maritime Museum.*

The storm hit, leaving mariners along the East Coast in peril from Maine to New Jersey. While numerous reports of ships stranded or disappearing began to surface over the following day, the fate of the *Pace* and the *Hanscom* remained a mystery. The December 1898 edition of the *New York Maritime Register* reported the *Pace* as "overdue," followed by several months of "missing" status.

The fifteen-year-old *Pace*, weighing in at 642 tons and measuring 161 feet, was owned by Garfield's father, Captain William Garfield, along with the Fisk brothers and several other citizens of West Dennis. Garfield had a wife and two children, along with five sisters and two brothers.

The Dennis Historical Society summed up the situation on the homefront in its December 1987 newsletter:

> *As the weeks went by, this sad fact is oft repeated. Fear has been expressed for the safety of the* Pace. *The worst is expected.*

The Nickerson family of Dennis Port was also distressed. Dannie Nickerson was the *Pace*'s first mate. He was described by the Dennis Historical Society as "a devout young man about whom his eulogist said, 'None knew him but to love him, none named him but to praise.' As his young wife cared for their eight-month-old son, surely she was able to keep hope alive for a time. But the truth must be faced."

As the days and weeks passed, any optimism for the *Pace*'s survival was fading fast. Then, in December 1899, some very unsettling news reached Dennis. As Gruzen reported, government divers "investigating navigational obstructions at the bottom of the seas off Montauk Point" discovered the *Pace* and the *Hanscom*. The *New York Maritime Register* relayed the gruesome details:

> *In both vessels the divers report that skeletons of men were found lashed to the rigging or to the rails of the vessels, and while there is nothing left of the flesh, it is thought that they can be recognized by the clothing.*

The Dennis Historical Society came to this conclusion from its research:

> *They had apparently fouled each other while scudding along before the sixty mile-per-hour winds of the Portland Gale. Lashed to the riggings of these ill-fated vessels were the skeletons of their crews. This was no doubt an emergency measure, taken to prevent the men from being washed overboard. The vessels must have collided so unexpectedly that the hapless seamen had no opportunity to even attempt to free themselves.*

A painting of the *James B. Pace* now hangs on the wall of the Dennis Maritime Museum in West Dennis, about a mile north of Nantucket Sound. Its description notes the now eternal connection between Garfield and Holmes:

> *What a twist of fate that the two captains who were such close friends should go to a watery grave together.*

OTHERS LOST NEAR PROVINCETOWN

In the days following the storm, Race Point in Provincetown saw plenty of wreckage washing ashore. Along with some of the wreckage of the *Portland*, remains of the vessels *Pentagoet* and *Addie E. Snow* were also found, fueling speculation that one of those ships collided with the *Portland*.

According to the website for the Stellwagen Bank Marine Sanctuary, the *Pentagoet*, under the command of Captain Orris R. Ingraham, left New York on November 24, heading for Rockland and then Bangor, Maine. Robert H. Farson wrote in his book, *Twelve Men Down: Massachusetts Sea Rescues*, that the *Pentagoet* was carrying a large cargo of freight, including Christmas toys.

The *Pentagoet* was last spotted off Truro by the steamer *Halifax* on Saturday night at about 6:00 p.m., according to the December 6, 1898 edition of the *Boston Daily Advertiser*. The vessel's crew of eighteen was never seen again.

Stmr. Pentagoet, Capt. O.R. Ingraham.
Lost in storm of November 2, 1878

The steamer *Pentagoet*, at one time a navy vessel during the Civil War, was lost off the Cape during the storm. *Stellwagen Bank Marine Sanctuary.*

According to the *Rockland Courier-Gazette* of December 3, 1898, Captain Ingraham's brother David Ingraham stated that his brother "had the utmost faith in the seaworthiness of the steamer, especially after he made a trip from Cape Cod to this port in a storm during which the Boston and Bangor steamers dared not venture out."

The December 7, 1898 edition of the *Boston Globe* reported that a red painted fly rail that fit the description of the *Pentagoet* was recovered at Race Point. Captain Ingraham's twin brother, Captain Otis Ingraham of the steamer *City of Bangor*, had given up all hopes for the *Pentagoet* at this point, believing that the steamer "broke her machinery during the gale and in helpless condition wallowed in the trough of the sea and soon foundered."

Originally built in Philadelphia in 1864 for the U.S. Navy, the vessel was first utilized as the *Moccasin* in the Civil War. After the war, it was transferred to the Revenue Marine Service and christened the *George M. Bibb*. It was later a customs service boat on the Great Lakes before its final incarnation as the freight steamer *Pentagoet*.

The four-masted *King Philip*, carrying coal from Baltimore, was on one of its regular runs to Portland but never made it. The vessel was within thirty miles of its destination as the storm kicked in but was likely driven back and forced on to the Peaked Hill Bars off Provincetown. A quarter board bearing the name *King Philip* came ashore near the Peaked Hill Bars Life-Saving Station.

According to William U. Swan's 1921 article in *Cape Cod Magazine*, the *King Philip* and the *Alicia B. Crosby* were both trying to reach Portland, with only the *Crosby* making port. A few beams and a small steam pump bolted on them were later found on the beach in Brewster. The number of the brass plate on the pump identified it as belonging to the *King Philip*, and this number enabled the widow of Captain A.A. Duncan to collect his life insurance.

The *King Philip* also had a war background, according to the December 1, 1898 edition of the *Boston Globe*. It was one of the first vessels chartered by the government during the Spanish-American War earlier that year to carry coal from Baltimore to the warships at Key West, Florida, and made a few trips with fuel to replenish the bunkers of the fleet.

BARGES CUT LOOSE, LOST

The tugboat *Mars*, missing for two days after the storm, finally turned up in Boston on November 29, but unfortunately without its barges. The boat's captain, identified by the *Boston Post* as "Captain Miles," was in Massachusetts

Bay at 1:00 a.m. on November 27, but the hurricane-force winds made it impossible for the tug to hold on to the *Delaware*, carrying six men, and the *Daniel I. Tenney*, with a crew of five. All eleven men later perished.

The captain signaled both boats to anchor. "There were then between Minot's Light and the lightship, and Captain Miles believed that could hold on, as they were both equipped with good tackle," the November 30 edition of the *Post* reported. High waves broke over the *Mars*, smashing the pilothouse windows, flooding the cabin and filling the lower part off the boat, until it was feared that the fires would be extinguished. At one time, the vessel was half full of water.

Miles and the *Mars* retreated eastward, anchoring off Wellfleet until weather conditions eased. "After much hard work and many starts the *Mars* found itself in a lull off the leeward side of Billingsgate Island," Fred Freitas and Dave Ball wrote in *Warnings Ignored!* "It was a mystery as to how that got there because of the deadly shoals which surrounded the island."

On the way back, he followed the beach all the way from Gurnet Light in Plymouth but could find no trace of the missing barges. They were later found off Cohasset.

Near Misses for Dennis Captains

"Captain Peleg Thacher was noted for his caution and his good judgment. This trait of character was a blessing to him many times, as in the gale of 1898," wrote Neva O'Neil in the July 15, 1938 edition of the *Yarmouth Register*. Thacher and the *James H. Hoyt* ventured out from Bass River on the morning of November 26, 1898. By the time they reached Highland Light in Truro, Thacher had second thoughts about continuing. "We are turning around and going back to Bass River," he told his mate. "This don't look good." It wasn't long before they were safely anchored back on Bass River.

Captain Prince Bearse of Centerville and the schooner *L.C. Ballard* of Barnstable also happened to be in the vicinity of Bass River on November 26 but did not sail, as the December 5, 1898 edition of the *Barnstable Patriot* noted.

Many others ventured out that Saturday and somehow returned, but some returned only after paying a substantial price.

SURVIVORS AT SEA

By some folks' rules, one is only a true Cape Codder when the family archives
trace back to the Mayflower, *or thereabouts. But Captain Allen S. Bragg*
became a genuine Cape Codder in an initiation that few, if any, Brewster-born
folks had undergone, and lived to tell the tale.
—*Joan Paine,* Cape Cod Masters of the Seas: Extraordinary Tales of
Brewster's Shipmasters and Packet Captains

D uring the second and third weeks of November 1898, Captain Allen
S. Bragg was on board the ship *Mary A. Tyler,* delivering valuable
cargo to various ports along the East Coast of the United States.
Only twenty-five years of age, Bragg, a native of North Carolina, had quickly
established himself on the high seas since leaving Graham Academy seven
years earlier. On November 28, after leaving Bath, Maine, his life changed
forever when the *Mary A. Tyler* broke apart during the storm in Cape Cod Bay.

From that point on, his life would be centered in Brewster, where Captain
Jeremiah Wixon and several other Brewster residents rescued Bragg and
his men from the shattered vessel. Six years later, Bragg married Wixon's
daughter, Margaret, at the senior captain's home on Stoney Brook Road.

Stormy conditions began shortly after the *Tyler* left port in Maine, and
the winds quickly reached hurricane force with driving sleet. Trying to
maintain the course for New York, the *Tyler* forged ahead. The captain's
daughter, Miriam C. Bragg, recalled her father's account of the rescue for
the Brewster Historical Society in 1971:

Grimly he and his men worked to keep their own ship afloat. Just before night fell as the terrifically high and pounding waters off Cape Cod, his boat broke in two. The forecastle, remaining just enough above water to allow the men to try, but in vain, to light a blaze however small, for warmth, by pouring kerosene on coal. They had a few water-soaked soda crackers, but they were too frozen and sick to eat. They tied themselves together with a rope and after hours of struggling with the wind and the icy deck managed to lash themselves to the mast. All during that frozen night of horror the wind whipped the mast into the sea—tossing it up and down, as though it were as more than a splinter, freezing them to it. Their clothes were iced to their bodies—they were vomiting and nearly unconscious. The wind abated somewhat toward morning and after daybreak they were sighted from shore.

Captain Wixon and the Brewster men launched a dory from shore, making their way through the icy water to the *Tyler*, and "threw a buoy to the shipwrecked men," according to Miriam Bragg.

The uninsured *Tyler*, owned by H.P. Havens, was built in Setauket, New York, in 1866 and weighed 195 tons. Captain Bragg reportedly told his daughter that "for a long, long time the tides brought in rolls of paper from his wrecked ship, which the natives gathered, dried and used."

Bragg grew up on Ocracoke Island in North Carolina, where Blackbeard the pirate was said to have met his demise, and obtained his navigator's license while still in school. His adventurous life at sea didn't end with the 1898 gale. Brewster historian Michael Pregot wrote in his book *Sea Captains*

Captain Allen S. Bragg, who died in 1956, is buried in Brewster, close to where his ship, the *Mary A. Tyler*, broke up in Cape Cod Bay during the storm. *Author's collection.*

of Cape Cod that Bragg "developed a wonderful business acumen and was seen as having a kindly demeanor," while becoming a successful trader in European markets.

During World War I, he was a lieutenant commander for the U.S. Navy, leading some of the largest transports of the conflict. During World War II, he worked for the government as a civilian in charge of a Michigan shipyard, which built small boats.

On the Cape, he was a member of both the Masonic Order and the Harwich Baptist Church and was a cranberry grower. "Service to his church and his local community were of utmost important to him," Pregot noted. Bragg's memory lives on at the Captains Golf Course in Brewster, where the second hole on the Starboard course is named for him.

HORATIO HALL

The steamer *Horatio Hall* of the Maine Steamship Company somehow "went through the hurricane of Saturday night and Sunday without a particle of damage to herself, arrived [in New York] looking as spick and span as she did the day she started out on her trial trip," according to the report from the *Portland Daily Press* during the first week of December in 1898. "There was not as much as a deck bucket missing from this handsome ship," the *Press* said.

As the *Portland* left Boston at seven o'clock on the night of November 26, the *Hall* departed Portland for New York an hour later. By the time it rounded Provincetown, heading along the shore of Cape Cod, just before midnight, the storm (which was actually two low-pressure areas colliding) had picked up in intensity. "I knew that we were in for a very bad night of it," Captain Albert Bragg told the *Press* upon reaching New York.

Hurricane-force winds were soon upon them, but "the *Hall* behaved splendidly," Bragg said. "I never knew of a vessel which stood the heavy seas as well as she did. Of course we shipped a little water, but not any great amount of it at a time."

By 3:00 a.m., the waves were running at a height never before witnessed by Bragg in his thirty-plus years on the high seas. The seas continued to rise, "fully ten feet above our flagstaff," Bragg said. Over the next few hours, they were on course, passing by Eastham and Chatham, not another vessel in sight.

"At 7 a.m. Sunday morning, we could not have been very far from the steamer *Portland*, which must have drifted down to about this point before she foundered, but we saw nothing of her," Bragg said.

The steamer *Horatio Hall*, under the command of Captain Albert Bragg, somehow survived the storm at sea. The *Hall* arrived in New York a day late. *Author's collection.*

Passing around Monomoy was not without its own set of challenges; the Pilgrims found this out in 1620 when the *Mayflower* nearly stranded there. *Pollock Rip Lightship* had drifted off course, and snow, accompanied by thunder and lightning, picked up again. By 2:00 p.m. Sunday, the *Hall* was safely anchored in Vineyard Sound near Falmouth.

The *Hall*, which was briefly reported as lost, reached New York a day late. On the return trip to Maine, the crew of the *Hall* kept an eye out for remains of the *Portland* while passing the Outer Cape but saw nothing. Bragg, who knew Hollis Blanchard, the *Portland*'s captain, referred to the lost mariner as "a brave man."

Bragg also still seemed amazed that the *Hall*, with about twenty people on board, fared as well as it did in the historic storm and added that "these passengers suffered not a little from sea sickness, but were at no time frightened or panic stricken."

The *Hall* continued to sail until its demise following a collision with the *H.F. Dimock* in Pollock Rip off Chatham in 1909. The March 29, 1909 edition of the *Hyannis Patriot* reported that Bragg "was weeping over the loss of the vessel he once commanded. Great tears rolled down the hardy old mariner's cheeks as he sadly admitted there was no hope of saving the 'good old ship.'"

EMMA M. DYER

As the storm was departing the Cape region, Daniel B. Gould of the Orleans Life-Saving Station was patrolling Nauset Beach. While he and his fellow surfmen had already found a few bodies, Gould also came across a bottle with a note. The *Emma M. Dyer* of Gloucester was in distress, the note said, and about to sink. Its spars and sails were gone. "The writer requested the finder to notify his wife, who lived at 92 Maplewood Ave., Gloucester," according to the November 30, 1898 edition of the *Boston Globe*. A few minutes later, Gould found the bow of a vessel with the name "Emma M."

The note proved to be true. A day later, "sixteen bronzed and weather-beaten seamen in oilskins stood on the forward deck of the Metropolitan steamship *Herman Winter*" in Philadelphia, ready to tell the story of how they returned to shore without their two-masted vessel, the *Emma M. Dyer*, which was lost six miles south of Cape Cod on November 28.

The Gloucester fishermen "were taken off the shattered and dismasted hulk of the vessel," according to the December 1, 1898 edition of the *New York Journal*, by the crew of the steamer *Herman Winter*. "The lifeboat of the *Herman Winter* and the two dories of the schooner were smashed in the rescue, but not a man in the fishing smack was lost," the *Journal* said.

The *Dyer*, weighing in at seventy-five tons, was returning from a successful fishing trip when the storm struck and was trying to reach Provincetown Harbor. The storm "came on to snow so thick that we could not see a dozen yards ahead and the wind came in terrific squalls," *Dyer* captain Otto Jansen told the *Journal*.

Throughout the night, the elements continued to pound the schooner, but somehow it remained dry below the deck. At eight o'clock Sunday morning, they spotted the steamer *Dorchester*. The *Journal* reported Jansen's story of the encounter:

> *I yelled to the captain that we were in danger of going ashore and wanted to be taken off. Captain Parker, of the* Dorchester, *made no reply, but the steamer circled us twice slowly and then steamed off on her course, leaving us to our fate.*

The *Emma M. Dyer* then let out the port anchor, only to have it snap within a half hour. The foremast was then lost, and the starboard anchor was released after it became tangled in the fore rigging. "We had to let out sixty fathoms of chain, and at last the weight of the chain tore loose the anchor, and it went to the bottom and held," Jansen said. From there, the situation only became worse, the captain said:

> *But the waves were making clean over us that night and the snow drove into our faces in blinding swirls that made it impossible to do more than hang on where we stood. There was no chance to display a signal of distress, and as for burning lights there was not a signal left dry on board, and the cabin was flooded. The decks were flooded, too, level with the bulwarks, most of the time. We hung there throughout the night.*

At 1:30 p.m. on Monday, November 28, the *Dyer* crew, lashed to what was left of the rigging, sighted the *Herman Winter*. Second mate Herbert Crowell of the *Winter* told the *Boston Globe* that "we took the *Winter* up as close as we could and heaved a line to the *Dyer*." However, the cables that were to be used in the rescue attempt snapped. A long struggle using the *Winter*'s lifeboat and the *Dyer*'s dories followed. "The *Winter* rolled like a drunken sailor when we got back to her, and it was a hazardous thing to approach her," Crowell said. When the *Dyer* crewmen were assured that a rescue was certain, they doused the schooner's cabin with kerosene and set it ablaze.

While the captain of the steamer *Dorchester* was identified as "Captain Parker," this later proved to be inaccurate, according to the December 6, 1898 edition of the *Cape Cod Item and Bee*:

> *Captain Parker was not on board the* Dorchester *at this time. He was at his home in Hyannis, and as no cars were running he could not get to Boston, and the* Dorchester *sailed without him, in charge of his mate. Captain Parker left Hyannis Tuesday and went through to Baltimore by rail, and joined his ship at that point.*

BOSTON HARBOR

As the *Portland* Gale raged over Cape Cod and the islands, the rest of the New England coast was also feeling its effects. Vessels were being tossed about the waters of Boston Harbor. "The storm probably struck no portion of the coast with greater power than in this vicinity, and the men of the Point Allerton Life-Saving Station were arduously engaged during the whole period," the U.S. Lifesaving Service noted.

Keeper Joshua James, *seated second from left*, and his crew from the Point Allerton Life-Saving Station in Hull were involved in the rescues of several Cape Codders in Boston Harbor. *U.S. Coast Guard.*

The Point Allerton Life-Saving Station, located along the southern reaches of Boston Harbor in Hull, was led by its seventy-two-year-old keeper, Joshua James. The Point Allerton skipper is recognized as a legend in lifesaving circles, saving more than five hundred people during his career. Among those stranded in Boston Harbor that weekend were sailors from Cape Cod.

There was little rest that night for James and his Point Allerton crew. Shortly after the rescue of a coal barge, the three-masted schooner *Calvin F. Baker*, captained by J. Parker Megathlin of West Dennis, struck a submerged ledge in the back of Little Brewster Island. Over the next two and a half days, three men from the crew of eight were lost.

Boston light keeper Henry Pingree was powerless to help the distressed men, as much of the island was covered by waves. James and company were unable to attempt a rescue until Sunday morning. The U.S. Life-Saving Service summary of the disaster follows:

> *All hands were driven to the rigging as the breakers swept over the ship.*
> *When the tide receded the men were able to find shelter under a small*

portion of the forward deck that had escaped the devouring seas. Every now and then, while the sailors were thus huddled together in their cramped and uncertain retreat, a tremendous wave would rush over the craft from stem to stern and drench them where they were, while the biting cold stiffened their garments with ice. Then the incoming tide would race them again to the rigging. In this way the seas pursued them from one part of the vessel to another, and witnessing the loss of three of their shipmates, they underwent the long, grim hours before their rescue.

During the day on Sunday, the men aboard the *Calvin F. Baker* were calling for help. According to historian Edward Rowe Snow's *Storms and Shipwrecks of New England*, the mother of one of the assistant keepers was so affected by the shock of hearing the frozen men calling for aid throughout that day and the following night that she died shortly afterward.

The first victim, according to the November 29, 1898 edition of the *Chatham Monitor*, was Burgess S. Howland of South Yarmouth, the ship's first mate. "His shipmates held on to him as long as they could, but he was finally washed away," the *Monitor* reported.

According to the *Monitor*'s account, the keepers at Boston Light made several attempts to shoot a line to the *Calvin F. Baker* but fell short. The second mate, whose identity is not clear in accounts of the wreck, attempted to save

The three-masted schooner *Calvin F. Baker*, captained by J. Parker Megathlin of West Dennis, struck a submerged ledge near Boston Light. *U.S. Coast Guard.*

his mates by swimming to shore with the line. "The second mate made the daring attempt to swim to Boston Light in the seething, hissing, mountainous seas," according to the December 5, 1898 edition of the *Barnstable Patriot*. "It was done against the protest of the captain, but with a 'If I am lost, it won't be but a few moments before the rest of you,' he plunged overboard to his death."

On Sunday morning, the Point Allerton Life-Saving Station crew engaged the tug *Ariel* to the area between the lighthouse and Great Brewster Island, according to Snow. The surfboat was then launched over "combers [that] were ominously breaking," according to the Life-Saving Service, and were soon next to the wrecked vessel. It was at this point that, according to Snow, it was discovered that the ship's steward, Willis Studley of Monument Beach, was dead. Megathlin hit Studley on the shoulder to awaken him, but the frozen body fell over. Out of the five survivors, the Life-Saving Service noted, Megathlin "was the only one not far gone." The agency concluded:

> *The scene was one no eyes could wish to dwell upon, and the Lifesavers hastened to flee the place. The living—but half alive—and the dead were quickly handed over into the surfboat, which was promptly pulled away to the tug that stood by to tow her home.*

Studley's wife, Abbie, along with his brother, Matthew, went to Hull a few days later to recover his body. The couple was married on Thanksgiving Day seven years earlier. Studley left behind two small children. According to the *Sandwich Independent*, Studley's "body was laid at rest beside the little one who passed on before."

Alfred F. Nickerson of Chatham was another Cape Codder pulled from the stormy surf of Boston Harbor that night, but his savior turned out to be someone very close to home. As Nickerson recalled for the *Cape Codder* in July 1947:

> *Lifesavers were there with lines as far as they could get out. One of them was Nathaniel Bearse. He lived in Chatham and he was one of my neighbors, but I didn't know it for a long time. He grabbed me.*

Nickerson was among the crew of *Coal Barge No. 1* of the Consolidated Coal Company, which was headed from Baltimore to Boston, carrying 1,600 tons of coal on the night of November 26, 1898.

The storm kicked into gear during the early evening as the barge passed Highland Light. Just outside Boston Light, the barge let its anchors go. "We didn't stay to anchor twenty minutes before she dragged both anchors," Nickerson recalled. "And we went ashore at Hull."

At Hull's Point Allerton Life-Saving Station, Joshua James and his crew were summoned. James and company had just completed the rescue of the *Henry R. Tilton*. By 11:00 p.m., they were at the site. James and his men attempted a breeches buoy rescue, but to no avail. At this point, the barge, battered by heavy surf, was breaking up. Rescuers then waded out to reach the vessel. Crewmen on the barge, stripped down to their underclothes, had retreated to the boat's pilothouse, but their haven broke free and was headed to shore. "We knew we'd have to swim for it," Nickerson said.

Accounts vary on the fate of the pilothouse, but Nickerson and his mates were pulled from the water. "We all stayed in the pilothouse until it was ripped off clean," he said. "We hung right to her when she went over and 'til she hit the bottom. Then we leaped into the sea."

Once ashore, heavy snow and hurricane-force winds prevented the rescuers from bringing the shipwreck victims to the station, "so they broke into a cottage," Nickerson said. "In the cottage they gave us a little whiskey and hot water. After a while the horse and wagon took us to the lifesaving station."

It would be different sets of circumstances for *Coal Barge No. 1* and the *Portland*, even though the two vessels nearly crossed paths at one point. "The *Portland* went out on Broad Sound," Nickerson said. "We went in through the Narrows. Nobody knows what happened to her."

Captain Benjamin Hawes, a Hyannis native known as "Gentleman Ben," somehow maneuvered his double-stacked steel tug, the *Eureka*, into Boston Harbor. *U.S. Coast Guard.*

Captain Benjamin Hawes, known as "Gentleman Ben," somehow maneuvered his double-stacked steel tug, the *Eureka*, and three coal barges into Boston Harbor on the night of November 26, 1898. The nineteen men aboard the tug and the barges survived, while one of the barges was stranded on Galloupe's Island in the harbor.

"In the blinding snow, he could not see far enough astern to identify barges, and he is in a quandary as to the two which went ashore on Galloupe's Island in an unexposed position," the November 28, 1898 edition of the *Boston Post* reported. The paper added that the *Eureka* lost a portion of its wheel "by striking some hidden obstruction."

When the storm hit earlier in the evening, the *Eureka* was halfway between the *Pollock Rip Lightship* off Chatham and Truro. Wellfleet historian Earle Rich, author of the book *Cape Cod Echoes*, asked Hawes why he didn't turn back. The captain, a Hyannis native, paused and then offered a carefully worded answer:

> *There's a lot you don't know yet, boy, about towing a string of barges. You have others to think of. I did think of trying to make Nauset Inlet at one time, but gave up the idea knowing my tail barge would never make it. I would much rather have gone down with them than to have been the only survivor.*

STEAMER *GLOUCESTER*

The *Portland* wasn't the only steamer to leave Boston Harbor on the night of November 26. Also heading out was the steamer *Gloucester* of the Merchants' & Miners' Transportation line, under the command of Captain Frank Howes.

The *Gloucester* was the only ship to pass safely through Vineyard Sound during the storm and arrived at Norfolk, Virginia, at 6:00 a.m. on November 28, right on schedule. "His handling of the *Gloucester* in that awesome storm won him practically universal commendation," wrote Edward Rowe Snow in his book *New England Sea Tragedies*.

According to the 1897 publication "Somerville Past and Present," Howes was born in Chatham in 1840, to a seafaring family. He married a local lady, Catherine Doane, and was the father of six children. On May 10, 1919, the *Yarmouth Register* noted that he became famous among the mariners of Boston as the first man to pilot a battleship into Boston Harbor at night, when he brought the *Missouri* through the upper channel for the Newport Shipbuilding Company.

Unlike the *Portland*, the *Gloucester* was relatively stable in the water. According to Art Millmore's *And the Sea Shall Have Them All*, "The *Gloucester* was fully loaded with freight, which put the heaviest weights way down in the bottom of the cargo holds, stabilizing the ship with a very low center of gravity."

Howes wrote about his adventure for Snow fourteen years after the storm, noting that he left Boston at 4:15 p.m. Northeasterly winds were already approaching gale force, he said, but he added, "I thought it would try it anyway." By 7:30 p.m., he was off his homeland of Cape Cod, fighting to stay offshore. A snow squall was raging, with winds approaching hurricane force.

The *Gloucester* passed *Pollock Rip Lightship*, nearly running over the Pollock Rip Shoals buoy, then on to Vineyard Sound. As the steamer approached Block Island, Rhode Island, winds were gusting to 110 miles per hour. Water from the high waves was rolling into the staterooms, and anchoring wasn't an option. Howes ventured ahead, hitting speeds of eighteen knots, all the while accurately calculating what locations were next—West Chop Light on Martha's Vineyard, Block Island and then Fire Island, New York. The December 6, 1898 edition of the *Chatham Monitor* offered this report:

> The Gloucester *sustained no damage of any importance, and while Captain Howes says the storm was one of the very worst in his experience, he adds that, being one of those who came through it safely, and with little or no damage to his craft, his experiences are not so thrilling as those which could be related by one who had been wrecked or who had narrowly escaped serious disaster.*

According to Edward Rowe Snow, the quartermaster of the *Gloucester* was talking to Ansel Dyer, quartermaster of the *Portland*, before both steamers left Boston. Upon his return to Boston, Howes was informed that Dyer's body was among those lost on the *Portland*.

RUTH M. MARTIN

The *Ruth M. Martin*, with a crew of twenty-three men captained by Michael Hogan, was fighting for its life on the morning of November 27, struggling to avoid the shoals in the high seas off Highland Light in Truro. After spotting what the crew thought may have been the *Portland* or the *Pentagoet* steamers, the *Ruth M. Martin* managed to ride up on the back shore of Provincetown, sustaining little damage. The December 3, 1898 edition of the *Boston Post* reported:

Last Saturday previous to the advent of the blizzard the schooner anchored back of Cape Cod where she held until the following day, when both cables parted and the craft stood offshore. An exciting time followed until she had sailed into Provincetown Harbor. Some of her crew had been banged around and were more or less injured, but none seriously. A heavy sea at one period in the gale slapped the vessel on the port side just abaft the fore rigging and caving in some of the bulwarks and heavy rail.

According to Fred Freitas and Dave Ball in their book *Warnings Ignored!*, Captain Hogan was able to beach his schooner near Provincetown, and on December 1, he was towed into Provincetown Harbor.

MERTIS H. PERRY

During the first week of December 1898, Frank H. Perry of Brewster was staying near the Brant Rock Life-Saving Station in Marshfield, looking after the schooner *Mertis H. Perry*, which was wrecked during the storm. Perry, a part owner of the vessel, named the schooner for his daughter, according to the December 5, 1898 edition of the *Barnstable Patriot*.

The *Mertis H. Perry* "was cast ashore two miles north-northwest of the Brant Rock Life Saving Station between 9 and 10 a.m. on November 27, 1898," according to the U.S. Life-Saving Service. Three men drowned and two died from exposure.

The schooner left Boston on November 21 with a crew of fourteen. Off Provincetown, with fifteen thousand pounds of fish, the *Perry* started back for Boston on November 26. After battling the storm all night, the boat was forced to "strike the beach somewhere and take their chances." Two men quickly perished—William Bagnall "gave up and died" from exposure, and then Captain Joshua Pike, of Nova Scotia, "had evidently become demented from his awful experience, for he abruptly picked up part of a dory which had been smashed in, and without saying a word, jumped overboard, and was not seen afterward," the Life-Saving Service reported.

The June 9, 2010 edition of the *Marshfield Mariner* looked back on the *Perry* wreck, with the reaction of part owner F.J. O'Hara. "She was driven in so close to the bluff that the men aboard of her were able to crawl out over the bowsprit and drop on the bluff itself," O'Hara said.

After the *Perry* struck the beach, the foremast swung in such a way that ten men were able to reach shore. However, Charles Forbes "was so prostrated that the survivors were obliged to leave him behind." They eventually reached a farmhouse, where they were taken in. Two of the farm hands were sent to look for Forbes, but they found him dead on the bluff. Two days later, Captain Pike's body was found on Gurnet Beach in Plymouth by one of the surfmen from the Gurnet Life-Saving Station.

Varuna

When the smashed bulwark planking of the pilot boat *Varuna* washed up in the marshes of East Barnstable following the storm, many assumed that the vessel was done for. So imagine the surprise of fellow mariners in Boston Harbor when it was towed back to Lewis Wharf by the Leyland line steamer *Philadelphian* on November 29.

Bulwark planking of the pilot boat *Varuna* washed up in the marshes of East Barnstable, but the crew of five survived the storm after being rescued at sea by a passing steamer. *Author's collection.*

The *Varuna* left Boston as the storm hit on November 26, 1898, and managed to stay offshore near Highland Light. "The *Varuna* was driven out past Cape Cod with frightful velocity and at times was near enough for the sailors to hear spray dashing against the beach," reported the November 30, 1898 edition of the *Boston Post*. The ship's mainsail was torn, the bulwarks and foresail carried away, the cabin was flooded and one of the canoes was damaged but quickly repaired, which Pilot Harry Petersen was able to utilize in boarding the *Philadelphian* thirty miles east of the Cape.

Captain William Fairfield, lashed to the wheel, suffered two broken ribs but pressed on. Tom Cunliffe, in his book, *Pilots: The World of Pilotage Under Sail and Oar*, wrote that Fairfield told the crew to "keep her headed up and make a straight wake; she is made of oak and copper and can stand it."

The *Varuna*, a sister vessel of the pilot boat *Columbia*, which wrecked off Scituate in the storm, was welcomed by cheers from the boats in Boston Harbor upon its arrival home. The crew also realized how fortunate they were, according to the *Boston Post*:

> *The pilot boat had some of the narrowest escapes on record from going ashore on Cape Cod, and she is almost a wreck. Pilot Petersen stated that neither himself, Captain McMillan, Captain William Fairfield, or the crew of five had expected ever to reach home.*

LOCKWOOD SAFE IN HYANNIS

The schooner *F.I. Lockwood*, under the command of Captain Claude Nickerson of Cotuit, had a narrow escape from the storm before finding safety near Hyannis Harbor on November 27, 1898, according to the December 5, 1898 edition of the *Barnstable Patriot*.

The *Lockwood* left Sullivan, Maine, on November 24 and made Provincetown the following day. On Saturday, November 26, the schooner encountered the snow and strong winds upon entering Nantucket Sound, passing Pollock Rip at 11:00 p.m. before anchoring. Nickerson said that there was no harbor on the coast that compared with Hyannis, and "it has been remarked by many coasting captains who speak in the highest terms of praise of our harbor."

Captain Ned Panno of Chatham, who was in charge of the barge *Moonbeam*, turned back for port in the nick of time before the storm. The *Chatham Monitor* of December 13, 1898, said that the *Moonbeam* left Newport

News, Virginia, on November 23 before dropping anchor in Hampton Roads until November 25, when it left for Boston. Panno and the *Moonbeam* didn't get far. He noticed that the vessel was leaking, and with the weather looking less than favorable, he returned to port that night. According to the *Monitor*:

> Had not Captain Panno turned back when he did he would surely have been caught in the storm when at its highest, and he and his men are now congratulating themselves on being alive, "with no sand in their ears."

LIGHTSHIPS GONE ASTRAY

In addition to the numerous lighthouses across Cape Cod, the U.S. Lighthouse Board also oversaw the operations of several lightships in the coastal waters. Even these usually stationary vessels weren't spared the fury of the storm.

Lightship No. 47, also known as the *Pollock Rip Lightship*, was taken on a ride from its usual position off Chatham all the way to Delaware. At 1:00 p.m. on November 27, 1898, the short-handed lightship, with three men on leave, broke free from its anchor and went adrift in the trough of the sea. According to Sylvester Baxter's account in the November 1899 edition

Lightship No. 47, also known as the *Pollock Rip Lightship*, broke free from its anchor during the storm and went adrift before being returned to the Cape sixteen days later. *Author's collection.*

This illustration from the *Boston Post* shows the *Pollock Rip Lightship* as it looked during its sixteen-day ordeal. *Author's collection.*

of *Scribner's Magazine*, "the lightship was hurled into the breakers of Stone Horse Shoal, where she struck bottom three times, but only lightly, as it happily chanced."

By the next day, the lightship, with its galley flooded, was thirty-five miles south of Nantucket. As the *Falmouth Enterprise* explained in its August 15, 1939 edition, Captain Judah Berry still couldn't get the craft under control, but kept his "siren shrieking." The *Boston Daily Advertiser* reported in its December 10, 1898 edition that "the ship was drawing eleven feet of water and there were rocky shoals on every side, ever which the sea showed white." Two days later, the lightship spotted the steamer *Switzerland* off the Delaware coast. The *Advertiser* recapped the rescue effort:

> She answered the lightship's distress signal and stood by. Captain Berry signaled that he wanted to be towed, and after some dangerous work in one of the small boats, the Switzerland got a line aboard and towed the lightship to Delaware breakwater.

Sixteen days later, on December 13, the *No. 47* was back at its post off the coast of Chatham. The *Hen and Chickens Lightship* also went adrift but returned to its post in at the entrance to Buzzards Bay under its own sail. The *Boston Daily Advertiser* reported that the lightship "drifted way beyond Newport, Rhode Island and up to Dutch Harbor [at Jamestown], a longer journey than she has ever taken before in a storm. She was replaced December 9."

The lightships survived. However, just to the south, in Vineyard Sound, between the Elizabeth Islands and Martha's Vineyard, similar horrors to those seen in Provincetown were being unleashed.

VINEYARD VIOLENCE

Never in all the time that I have been at sea have I seen
such scenes as I have just been through.
—Thomas Mullen of the schooner J.D. Ingraham,
as told to the Portland Daily Press, *November 30, 1898*

To the south of Cape Cod, about seven miles from Falmouth, lies the island of Martha's Vineyard. While separated by the waters of Vineyard Sound, the island and the Cape have much in common. In the case of the *Portland* Gale, it was an eerily similar scene at the harbors in Provincetown and Vineyard Haven.

The November 29, 1898 edition of the *Boston Globe* summed up the situation accurately with its headline, "Tossed Like Toys," followed by this description:

> *Sunday was the most eventful day that Vineyard Haven has known for forty years. From early morning until late at night the weather about this port was strewn with wreckage, and the vessels were constantly driven ashore, many of them to be dashed to pieces.*

All told, nearly fifty coasters were thrown around the harbor, formerly known as Holmes Hole, with half of them washing ashore. Ten men drowned. A British schooner was driven into the wharf near the Seamen's Bethel. Two schooners carrying lime took on water and went up in flames. As the *Boston Post* described the scene in the December 2, 1898 paper:

CENE IN VINEYARD HAVEN WHEN THE VESSELS WHICH FIRST PARTED THEIR CABLES BEGAN TO
DRIFT DOWN ON THE FLEET, CARRYING DESTRUCTION TO EVERYTHING BEFORE THEM.

Severe weather in Vineyard Haven Harbor caused several vessels to break free, leading to a
destructive scene, as depicted in this illustration from the *Boston Post*. *Author's collection.*

> *Frightful scenes connected with the recent storm will live for years in the
> memories of the people here. There were many things which those who saw
> them will never forget.*

The fury of the storm began to intensify around four o'clock on the
morning of November 27. At this point, Captain Soule of the three-
master *Hamilton*, carrying a load of coal from Perth Amboy, New Jersey, to

Portland, was just outside the harbor with two anchors out. As heavy snow picked up, the three-master *Newburgh* was driven about twenty feet from the *Hamilton* before striking the wharf. The *Thomaston* struck the *Hamilton* with its foremast, and the *Hamilton* dragged its anchor, according to Captain Soule's description in the *Falmouth Enterprise*:

> *Two other schooners fouled us. Together we were carried shoreward before the wind and sea. Four of us struck together. Three drifted off, hit a coal, barge and grounded again. Seas swept our deck. With my four men I climbed to the rigging. Hours later a volunteer crew from the shore took us off.*

According to the *Boston Post*'s December 2, 1898 edition, that volunteer crew consisted of "Messrs. Isaac Norton, Frank Golart, and Alvin Cleveland." The trio patched up a fourteen-foot dory and ventured out to the *Hamilton* and, "in the teeth of the howling gale," pulled all four men off the vessel. "These three men risked their lives to try to save others," the *Post* said. "Too much praise cannot be given these brave men for their heroic act." George Wiseman, author of *They Kept the Lower Lights Burning*, also included the names of Stanley Fisher and F. Horton Johnson among the rescuers.

Captain Wentworth of the tug *Robert Lockhart* led a rescue of the sunken three-masted schooner *Leona M. Thurlow* of Bath, Maine, with a cargo of paving stone. Four men joined him in rescuing six sailors from the rigging of the stranded vessel. The *Boston Post* opined, "Captain Wentworth is entitled to much praise for towing the boat down to the wrecks, as no other boat in the harbor would take the risk."

The *Hamilton* also collided with the schooner *M.E. Eldridge* of Dennis, bound from Albany for Boston, with a cargo of clay, according to the *Chatham Monitor* of November 29, 1898. Captain Roland Kelley's vessel went ashore near the steamboat pier at the west side of the harbor. It was dismasted, and the hull was badly damaged.

Two lime schooners from Rockland, Maine, the *Bertha E. Glover* and the *E.G. Willard*, found themselves looking to anchor in the harbor. The *Glover* took on water, causing the lime to ignite. The crew attempted to extinguish the flames, but to no avail. The ship continued to smolder, with the fire finally dying out on December 19, wrote Chris Baer in the *Martha's Vineyard Times* from October 26, 2019. Across the harbor, the *E.G. Willard* caught fire as well.

Wiseman wrote that the men of the *Willard* had to decide between drowning or burning. In what seemed to be a worsening situation, the schooner *J.D. Ingraham* was one of many vessels on the loose, heading straight toward the

Willard. Thomas Mullen, one of the sailors from the *Ingraham*, gave this account, which appeared in the *Portland Daily Press* on November 30, 1898:

> *A Rockland lime schooner whose anchors let go about the same time as ours did, came down on us and it was mighty luck for those on board of her that she did. She was on fire and the peril of her crew was great[er] than the danger we were in. When the two vessels fouled, all on board the Rockland schooner jumped aboard the* Ingraham. *They had no more than struck the deck than the two hulks broke apart and each vessel went on its own course to destruction.*

Upon his departure from Vineyard Haven after the storm, Mullen also made the newspapers aware of some grievances that he had with the rescue efforts in the harbor:

> *The manner in which men were allowed to die was scandalous. There were five big able towboats in the harbor and there was nothing in God's heavens to prevent them from getting to the windward of vessels which had men perishing in the rigging and dropping boats to them. Men died after the sea had quieted down so that small boats could go out and we were forced to see them die.*

The Seamen's Bethel on the Vineyard Haven wharf was nearly hit by the *Newburgh*. According to the account provided by Reverend Madison Edwards in Wiseman's book, the Seamen's Bethel "reeled to and fro" before the near miss. The Seamen's Bethel became a host for dozens of shipwrecked sailors over the next several days. In 1983, Gratia Harrington, who was thirteen at the time of the storm, told Linsey Lee of the Martha's Vineyard Museum that about seventy-five men were provided with accommodations and food. The account given by Edwards estimated that number to be closer to one hundred. The entire length of the Seamen's Bethel's reading room was filled with straw for sleeping accommodations at night and with long tables for meals during the day. The Woman's Christian Temperance Union took in those the Seamen's Bethel couldn't accommodate, while many citizens opened their homes to the stranded sailors. During the week after the storm, the WCTU and Vineyard Haven women of the Relief Corps hosted dinners for the men. The Seamen's Bethel was also the site for a memorial service for those lost in the harbor, conducted by Reverend Alfred Fairbrother.

In Cottage City (Oak Bluffs), the schooner *Island City* came ashore, so close to the wharf "that islanders could see her in the blizzard Sunday morning," the *Falmouth Enterprise* of August 15, 1939, recalled. Several men took to a dory to try to rescue a sailor lashed to the masts, but the boat capsized and the rescuers swam back to shore. That sailor eventually perished. According to Wiseman's account from Edwards, Fred James and Manuel Chaves nearly perished in the rescue attempt. Two other men died, and their bodies washed ashore. The *Boston Post* of December 2, 1898, had this report:

> *One of the men was seen hanging from the rigging by his heel, head downward. The bodies were picked up on the beach. With help close at hand they gradually froze and dropped, one by one.*

The steamer *Gate City* from Boston was thought to be missing after the storm but arrived at Savannah, Georgia, after being badly lashed by the waves. The *Barnstable Patriot* reported on December 5, 1898, that the *Gate City* anchored for thirty hours off Vineyard Haven to escape the force of the gale. The steamer lost some sails and several small boats, but no passengers were injured.

Stanley Fisher and F. Horton Johnson were recipients of gold medals from the government. The medals were presented one year later at the Baptist Church in Vineyard Haven. Wiseman also quoted the *Vineyard Gazette*, pointing out the tribute that the paper paid to Edwards, who also assisted the rescuers in their mission:

> *He knows the bliss of reward that comes from doing for others. For weeks Mr. Edwards gave himself for the comfort and entertainment of the unfortunate shipwrecked men.*

SIX LOST NEAR LOBSTERVILLE

On the morning of December 1, surfman Sylvanus Calhoun of the Gay Head Life-Saving Station arrived in Vineyard Haven, bound for South Orleans. Calhoun was on his way to the Cape for medical treatment after suffering an internal injury while attempting to launch a surfboat during the rescue of men from the schooner *Amelia G. Ireland* in Menemsha Bight.

Calhoun delivered horrible news to newspaper reporters at Vineyard Haven, informing them that one man perished in the *Ireland* disaster, while five more died nearby aboard the schooner *Clara Leavitt* when it went to pieces shortly after striking the sandbar. The Gay Head men were continually on duty from 11:00 p.m. on November 26 until 5:00 p.m. on November 28.

Surfmen from the Gay Head Life-Saving Station lit Coston flares as a signal to two distressed schooners that help was on the way. *Sturgis Library Archives.*

The *Boston Post* of December 2, 1898, described it as "one of the most thrilling stories furnished by lifesavers in this vicinity in many years, and it also disposes a persistence rarely equaled by members of such crews."

The two schooners were both anchored in Menemsha Bight early in the evening of November 26, 1898, but were soon in trouble as the storm set in. At about 10:00 p.m., Surfman Francis Manning was about a mile and half into his patrol, just north of Lobsterville, when he spotted the flash of a torch around Dogfish Bar, a shoal extending out on the westerly side of Menemsha Bight. He was able to make out the detail of a three-masted schooner in trouble and lit a Coston flare as a notice that the vessel was seen and that aid would be on the way.

Keeper Nehemiah Hayman, who was able to obtain the services of a yoke of oxen from a nearby farm, and his crew were soon on the scene. By 11:00 p.m., wreckage from the *Clara Leavitt* was washing ashore. One man, clinging to a fragment, was driven in and rescued. He was hurried to the station. A second torch, this one from the *Ireland*, was spotted and a boat launch was attempted, but the boat ended up going in the wrong direction, according to the Life-Saving Service report:

> *Some conception of the terrific power of the wind at this time may be gained from the fact that the surfboat was blown bodily across the entire beach, falling into a pool of water under the bank at least seventy-five yards distant.*

Six men from the *Amelia G. Ireland* were rescued by Gay Head lifesavers, utilizing a breeches buoy, after thirteen attempts. *Sturgis Library Archives.*

The rescue attempts resumed at dawn, this time with a Lyle gun, but twelve line shots to the boat came up short. Seven more attempts with the surfboat followed. An eighth attempt was met with success, and despite nearly capsizing, six men were rescued and taken to the station. Surprisingly, another survivor, Philo J. Sparrow, showed up at the door of Charles H. Ryan, the Life-Saving Service reported:

Seaman Philo J. Sparrow went overboard with the foremast, but managed to lay hold of a floating stanchion which buoyed him up until, in some marvelous manner, he found himself on the shore. On his hands and knees he dragged himself across the beach, making no outcry and undiscovered by anybody. Finding the road, he followed it to the house of Charles H. Ryan, where he was kindly cared for.

Among those lost on the *Clara Leavitt* was its captain, fifty-year-old James Lombard, who was at the helm of the ship substituting for his older brother, Benjamin Lombard, of Portland. The younger Lombard "lived in Wellfleet, where two daughters, the oldest about twenty years old, and a widow survive him. He was a skillful seamen well known to Portland," the *Portland Daily Press* reported on December 5, 1898.

ADDIE SAWYER

Yet another shipwrecked sailor was washed ashore on the beach at Martha's Vineyard and managed to find his way to shelter. Seaman Herbert Tapley of the schooner *Addie Sawyer* had the stamina to struggle—wet, chilled and tired—for two miles up a climbing road until finding shelter. Upon his arrival at the home on the hill, he managed the strength to utter the words, "Get the other fellows," according to the *Falmouth Enterprise*'s August 15, 1939 edition. His shipmate, Warren Dudley, also made it to shore. He was found unconscious on a road. No one was able to save "the other fellows," as the bodies of Captain Norwood, Cook Anzever and Seaman Lander Ashley were found frozen in the surf.

The *Sawyer* anchored just off Falmouth on the night of November 26, but the following afternoon, the anchor chains finally gave way. After briefly striking bottom in Vineyard Sound, the vessel, taking on water, finally struck the beach just west of Cedar Tree Neck. The five men were clinging to the deckhouse until the waves took it, fouling the overturned masts. The men clutched floating timbers from the deck load of lumber.

THREE WRECKS

The schooners *Queen Hester*, *Vivian* and *Clara C. Baker* struck near Gay Head, and seven men were drowned, the *Boston Globe* reported in its December

1, 1898 edition. The vessels went to pieces on the rocks where the steamer *City of Columbus* perished several years earlier. According to the *Globe*, the Gay Head Life-Saving Station crew "succeeded in rescuing nineteen. Seven, however, perished before assistance could reach them."

Fairfax Stranded

The three-thousand-ton steamer *Fairfax*, heading from Norfolk, Virginia, was a casualty of the storm, wrecking on Sow and Pigs Ledge off Cuttyhunk Island on November 27, 1898.

It turned out to be a blessing for all on board. All of the passengers were rescued. Being stranded on the ledge ended up being a much better option than being at sea. According to the *Falmouth Enterprise*, "one of the passengers reported she had slept much better on the Cuttyhunk rocks than the night before when the *Fairfax* fought the hurricane at sea."

The *Fairfax* approached the area of Block Island, Rhode Island, at 4:00 p.m. on November 27, heading for the Sow and Pigs Lightship. Another snow squall rolled in, obscuring all vision ahead of the steamer. The *Boston Daily Advertiser* of November 30, 1898, reported "the *Fairfax* passed the lightship to port when she should have been on the starboard. Those on the vessel did not hear the whistle of the lightship and all the time the sea continued to grow rougher."

The steamer began taking on water, extinguishing its flames below. The sea was breaking over the *Fairfax* after it struck bottom, but "the bottom proved to be level, and the *Fairfax* treated on an even keel," according to the *Advertiser*.

The Cuttyhunk Life-Saving Station spotted the steamer's debacle, but Captain Johnson of the Fairfax determined that the vessel was safe, according to the *Enterprise*:

> *I was rather loathe to fly distress signals. Cuttyhunk coast guards spotted us at 11 p.m. Sunday. I burned a Coston light but was careful to avoid giving any danger signal. They knew we were all right and didn't come off until morning.*

The Metropolitan line steamer *H.M. Whitney*, bound for New York for Boston, also spotted the wreck during the night and remained close by. The *Whitney* ended up taking one passenger, while the rest of the passengers

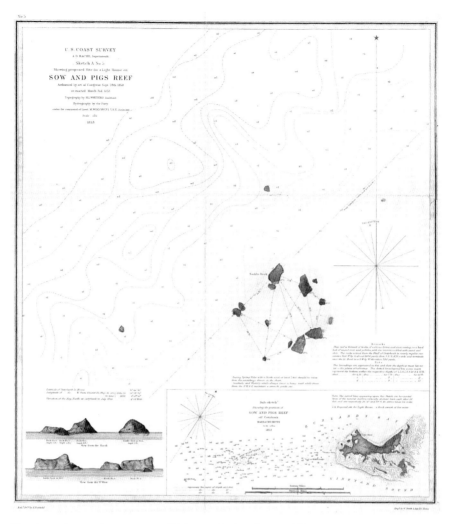

The three-thousand-ton steamer *Fairfax* wrecked on Sow and Pigs ledge in Vineyard Sound, off Cuttyhunk Island. *U.S. Coast Survey.*

boarded the tug *James Hughes Jr.* Captain Johnson abandoned the steamer but left his flag as a warning to keep wreckers off. A few hours later, he returned to attempt salvage operations, but the vessel was beyond repair. M. & M.T. Company, the *Fairfax*'s owners, followed with a first in legal actions in Massachusetts, bringing proceedings in U.S. District Court for limitation of liability and publication of abandonment of the wreck. The seven-year-old steamer was legally abandoned and eventually blown up, but not before much of the cargo, including a piano, was removed, according to the *Falmouth Enterprise*. The piano then entered the entertainment business:

> *A magnificent Chickering piano shared the billing with "Female Rope Skippers" and Ferrer's "educated rats" at the Boston Nickelodeon in the spring of 1899. It was a dime museum attraction to be featured with girls in bloomers, sixty trained rats and Miss Viola Jerome's female minstrels.*

Lunet Lost in Tarpaulin Cove

The three-masted schooner *Lunet*, carrying a load of coal from New York to Bangor, Maine, with a seven-man crew, was driven ashore along the sheltered confines of Naushon Island's Tarpaulin Cove. Naushon Island is one of the Elizabeth Islands chain, located just to the southwest of Woods Hole.

The *Portland Daily Press* reported on December 3, 1898, that the 197-ton vessel came into the harbor on Saturday prior to the storm, with the crew coming ashore and visiting the local post office. The *Lunet* was close to shore, with about one-third of the masts out of the water. "Owing to heavy seas, her crew could not have escaped," the *Press* added.

The Massachusetts Board of Underwater Archaeological Resources provided this description of the *Lunet*'s loss:

> *A change in wind direction from the northeast, accompanied by a blinding snowstorm, put the schooner in a dangerous position. Its proximity to the rocks and the reduced visibility prevented it from sailing further into the harbor. If its anchors could not withstand the strain of the seventy mile-per-hour gusts, the vessel would certainly be destroyed. Suddenly, the anchor chain parted and* Lunet *was flung across the reef at the southwestern entrance to the cove. The force of the impact tore its bottom out. Filling quickly the schooner sunk in sixty feet of water on the Sound side of the reef.*

In the summer of 1961, divers discovered what the August 8, 1961 edition of the *Falmouth Enterprise* suggested may be the remains of the *Lunet*.

The *Press* also reported on November 30, 1898, that "eleven vessels went ashore on Cuttyhunk and were badly wrecked."

While Martha's Vineyard spent the next several weeks getting back to normal, an island native would be serving in a pivotal role for recovery efforts on Cape Cod.

THE MEDIA
AND THE MEDICAL EXAMINER

The annals of this voracious beach! Who shall write them, unless it were a
shipwrecked sailor? How many have seen it only in the midst of danger and
distress, the last strip of earth which their mortal eyes beheld.
Think of the amount of suffering which a single strand has witnessed?
The ancients would have represented it as a sea-monster with open jaws, more
terrible than Scylla and Charybdis.
—Henry David Thoreau, Cape Cod

During the weeks following the loss of the *Portland*, dozens of bodies washed ashore from Provincetown to Monomoy. When word of the fatalities reached Boston and beyond, family members began to flock to the Cape in search of loved ones.

When the bodies were recovered from the beaches, the first stop was the office of the Cape's medical examiner, Dr. Samuel T. Davis of Orleans.

According to his obituary in the April 28, 1919 edition of the *Barnstable Patriot*, Davis, a native of Martha's Vineyard, was "remembered by older newspaper men for his great work during the storm of 1898 in which the steamer *Portland* was lost. During the disaster [he] had sixty-five newspaper reporters in his office or with him traveling as he hurried from one town to another, as the bodies were washed ashore."

Davis settled in Orleans in 1878, staying there for thirty years. He was appointed as the local medical examiner in the summer of 1898, just in time for the deadliest storm in Cape Cod history. Davis and his wife left Orleans

This illustration from the *Boston Post* shows Dr. Samuel T. Davis showing the body of a *Portland* victim to family members for identification. *Author's collection.*

in 1909, moving back to the Vineyard to serve as the medical examiner for the second district of Dukes County. He died ten years later, but his work during the *Portland* Gale wasn't soon forgotten, as the *Portland Daily Press* wrote in its December 1, 1898 edition:

> *Dr. Davis is a most untiring official. His district embraces all of that dreary Cape Cod shore along which every hour finds the body of another victim of the terrible storm coast by the sea.*

Davis had a tough task ahead of him. He reassured a reporter from the *Press* that he would do all in his power to preserve the bodies of all those found and identify them when possible.

For those searching for loved ones, Davis requested photographs "with a full description as to age, color of hair and eyes, whether the person wore a beard or mustache, if so, of what shade, marks upon the body, jewelry of any kind, if worn, clothing and its description…a full complete description to accompany all photographs and these must be attached to the picture in some way."

"Letters have been pouring in to me since Tuesday at the rate of nearly a hundred a day," Davis told the *Boston Post*. "Their requests for information tell of the tremendous sorrow the entire New England states are weighed down under." Conditions on the Cape following the storm didn't help matters. There was no telegraph service, and train service was limited. The only local hotel was packed.

Davis urged that the authorities move all bodies to Boston as soon as possible, which was accomplished "with the assistance of the state police and undertakers Mayo and Steele," the *Post* said. This created quite a hectic scene at the Orleans train station, the *Post* reported:

> *Carts of all descriptions were hurrying to the station with the boxes containing bodies. One wagon was a small hay wagon, while the others were all that could be asked to make up a specimen of a country barnyard. The drivers were very much awake, and the lumbering courses made better time than the law of Orleans allows, but the law breaks the law.*

The *Post* reported that Davis had "every part of the Cape covered, and he is notified very soon after a body is discovered." Within two weeks, most of the bodies had been recovered. The process started immediately after the disaster had been confirmed. Chief Rufus Wade of the state police and three other officers were authorized by Massachusetts governor Roger Wolcott to ship the bodies to Boston, the *Barnstable Patriot* reported on December 5, 1898. While the authorities were busy implementing their plans, the local media was wasting no time in obtaining as many details as possible.

Frank Stanyan of the *Boston Globe* broke the story with the first list of identified victims from the *Portland*. *Department of Special Collections and University Archives, W.E.B. Du Bois Library, University of Massachusetts Amherst.*

One of the reporters who sought out Davis immediately was Frank Stanyan of the *Boston Globe*. Stanyan, sent to Orleans along with another reporter and a sketch artist, broke the story with the first list of identified victims from

The Shattuck House in Orleans, shown here in the early twentieth century, became the headquarters for newspaper reporters on Cape Cod after the storm. *Author's collection.*

the *Portland*—by way of the French Cable Station undersea cable between Brest, France, and Orleans, operated by the French Telegraph Cable Company, or Cie Francaise des Cables Telegraphiques.

According to a tribute plaque presented to the French Cable Museum in 2018 by the Institute of Electrical and Electronic Engineers, the French Cable "provided communication between Europe and North America without intermediate relaying. In a remarkable feat of oceanic engineering, the cable was laid in the deepest waters of the Atlantic Ocean between Brest and Orleans. When completed in 1898, it spanned 3,174 nautical miles, making it the longest and heaviest cable in service."

It was at the Orleans station that Stanyan, who had spent two days scouring the town and beach along with Dr. Davis, had his story ready to go. Upon his return to the press headquarters at the Shattuck House in Orleans, Stanyan was informed that the lines between Barnstable and Orleans were down due to another storm. While the other reporters adjourned for dinner and drinks, Stanyan pondered as to how he would get his list of victims to the *Globe*. He headed back out and soon found himself near a building where he could hear the click of a telegraph key. In he went, finding out that it was indeed a telegraph station—the French Cable Station. As William U. Swan wrote for the December 30, 1928 edition of the *Boston Journal*:

As the cable station at Orleans had been doing very little business because of the failure of the telegraph line into New York, Superintendent [Hugh] Osborne, an Englishman in charge of a French cable, welcomed the newspaperman, threw open his office to copy writers and played the host to perfection.

The French Cable, which ran along the floor of the Atlantic Ocean, began operations in the mid-nineteenth century and moved its Massachusetts base from Duxbury to the Three Sisters Lighthouses in North Eastham in 1879. The station was moved again to Orleans in 1891. Forty-eight-year-old Hugh Osborne, referred to as "one of the best read and best informed men in Orleans" by the March 19, 1910 edition of the *Yarmouth Register*, had been the Cape's French Cable superintendent since 1885 and served in that capacity until his death in 1916. From this site, the *Portland* list was transmitted by Osborne in a most unusual way, as Alton H. Blackington detailed in his book, *Yankee Yarns*:

In a matter of seconds, the message sped from Orleans, on Cape Cod, to St. Pierre and Miquelon, then under the wild, dark Atlantic Ocean to Brest, France…from Brest to London, and from London via British Postal Service to Ireland, then, roughly, 2,500 miles to Canso, Nova Scotia, and down the storm-swept coast of New England into Boston.

The French Cable Station in Orleans was operated by the French Telegraph Cable Company. *Author's collection.*

Hugh Osborne, *first row, fourth from left*, was the superintendent of the French Cable Station in Orleans. *French Cable Station Museum, Orleans, Mass.*

Frank Sibley, who would later work for the *Globe*, was a twenty-six-year-old part-time reporter for the *Boston Journal*. The *Portland*'s only manifest went down with the steamer, so Sibley went to great lengths to obtain a list of names at the Portland Steam Packet Company in Boston. At the crowded office, Sibley offered to answer the phone, fielding the numerous calls coming in from concerned relatives and friends. After several hours of this, he managed to build up a lengthy passenger list.

The next morning, after Sibley and Bill Feeney of the *Boston Herald* spent the night there, C.F. Williams of the packet company arrived, saying that he hired a tug, the *Dudley Pray*, to go to the Cape to obtain news about the *Portland* and extended the invitation for the two reporters to tag along. When the tug rounded Long Point, wrecked vessels were spotted near Wood End. As they spotted the *Acushnet*, the tug approached. The captain yelled out, "Any news of the *Portland*?" "Sank last Sunday on Peaked Hill Bars," was the response. "Lots of her wreckage but all hands lost!"

They wanted to go ashore, but the captain, insisting that he had obtained the news he was seeking, refused. On the way back, they spotted two tugs bringing reporters to the Cape, much to their chagrin. Sibley still had his exclusive story from the day before, while the frustrated Feeney took some consolation from the heroic efforts of his fellow *Herald* correspondent, Charles F. Ward of Chatham.

Ward, described by Blackington as "a modest little man of Chatham," was known as "district man" for the *Boston Herald*. He was highly respected in local journalism circles, as the *Yarmouth Register* had this description of his skills on January 3, 1891:

> *Charles F. Ward is a quiet, unassuming gentleman, who has a keen eye for news, and his ability has attested to this fact on frequent occasions. His reports are concise and do not contain that superfluity of words which render them bungling and unreadable. He has many firm friends of the fraternity on the Cape.*

Thirty years old at the time of the storm, Ward spent most of his days wandering the Cape in his horse and buggy, gathering various news items, only to see a small percentage of these make it into print. The *Herald* had a fondness for printing his shipwreck stories, so Ward had a reliable network of friends across the Cape who would call him whenever they spotted a wreck.

On November 28, most of the lines of communication on the Cape were down, so Ward and his buggy ventured through the snowy and muddy roads to Hyannis, where he filled up three notebooks with storm stories in just a few hours. His efforts over the phone were turning up empty, but he managed to get a telegraph response from Isaac M. Small at Highland Light in Truro. The message offered up some short details of weather conditions and damage reports, followed by the news of the likely demise of the *Portland*, noting that the steamer may have wrecked on Peaked Hill Bars off Provincetown. The note concluded by saying, "Have much wreckage including tonnage board marked 2283. Looks like *Portland*. Not sure."

Ward checked in with a friend in Hyannis who kept a "ship's register." A retired mariner sitting with his friend said that he heard that two steamers were struggling off Peaked Hill. The ship's register confirmed the tonnage.

What followed was one of the most enduring efforts by a journalist to file his story. In *Scribner's Magazine*, Sylvester Baxter wrote, "[A]ppreciating that he was the exclusive possessor of news of transcendent importance, he was determined to get it Boston as best he might." At 6:30 p.m. on Monday, he went to the Hyannis railroad yard, "where a work train was making up to do a repair job up the Cape," in Blackington's words. The train left with Ward on board in the caboose. He fell asleep but woke up after the train stopped suddenly in Sandwich. The tracks were flooded. A small house was floating in this flooded area.

Ward finally reached Sandwich village around daybreak and found his way to a farmer's house. Phone lines were still down, the farmer said, but he offered the wayward reporter one of his horses. This got him to Buzzards Bay in time for the first train to Boston since the storm began. On the train, another reporter sat next to him, talking about what news items he had from the storm. Ward kept his "scoop" to himself.

The train reached Boston by 11:00 a.m. In another half hour, he made it through snowdrifts, stopping every few minutes to catch his breath. When he finally staggered up the stairs to the *Herald* office, someone yelled out that the *Portland* was safe in Provincetown Harbor. Still, he said nothing. Staggering through the busy newsroom, Ward finally collapsed on a desk. The editor of the *Herald* was hovering over him, ready to revive the exhausted reporter with a bottle of brandy.

Ward woke up, giving the editor his news and then passed out. The editor called the Portland Steamship Company office to confirm the tonnage. "We're getting out an extra!" the editor barked.

After a steak dinner at a Boston hotel, Ward sat back and enjoyed hearing the sounds of the local newsboys hawking the papers with his front-page story. It also won him lots of notoriety, according to the *Chatham Monitor* of December 13, 1898:

> *Take your hat off to Mr. Charles F. Ward of Chatham,* Boston Herald *correspondent, who made a big effort and "beat the town" with accurate news of the loss of steamer* Portland. *It was a big beat for the enterprising* Herald *and Ward was presented with $500.*

At around the same time that Sibley and Feeney were dispatched to Provincetown, the *Portland Daily Press* sent its reporter to the Cape tip aboard the revenue cutter *Woodbury*, searching for any evidence of the *Portland*. The *Press* reported that two other boats had arrived from Boston filled with newspapermen. "They were interviewing every one who had had anything to say and trying to get together some kind of a story on the disaster," the *Press* said. Many hired horse and carriage teams for transportation, especially to the desolate lifesaving stations in Provincetown and Truro. The trek was described by the *Press* as "a long and tedious" three-mile journey over the sand to the Peaked Hill Bars Life-Saving Station. Approaching the beach, "the thunder of the surf could be heard, booming out its solemn dirge over the dead," the *Press* reporter wrote.

Wandering the beaches of Provincetown, the *Press* reporter noted that two trunks came ashore, one marked "Madge Ingraham" and the other with the name of "L.C. Chase, 129 Washington St., Boston."

The reporter was hunting on the beach for a purser's book or some other record that might indicate the number of passengers but found nothing.

Back in Provincetown, Boston reporters were interviewing anyone who could tell them anything for a story. Many of the reporters worked all night, running about the town and driving over the rough roads of the Cape trying to find information.

By the next morning, a train had come into Provincetown for those seeking information on bodies lost. Among them was Fred Hooper of Portland, who had traveled all night from Boston, the *Press* reported. His father and his brother were passengers on the *Portland*. Hooper had a long trip, which included being transferred to wagons around big washouts in the road, in one place riding five or six miles over the sand dunes. He had to get out and stand in the rain and snow many times to allow the wagon to be hauled out of the deep sand. He reached Provincetown, hoping to find the bodies of his father or brother, but could not identify any of the corpses there. Hooper walked twelve miles of beach with the Life-Saving Service men in what proved to be a fruitless search. He went to Orleans and "then took a team and drove to Chatham to see two more bodies which had been cast up there

The revenue cutter *Woodbury* was dispatched from Portland, Maine, to search for the steamer *Portland* in Massachusetts Bay. *U.S. Coast Guard.*

by the sea." A day after departing the Cape, his father's body washed ashore and was recovered by the surfmen from the Orleans Life-Saving Station. Many others found themselves searching town after town for loved ones, wondering if they would have to make repeated trips to the Cape.

Many reporters and those seeking relatives took a long train ride from Provincetown to Orleans, which took three hours due to the washed-out train tracks in Truro.

On Wednesday night, November 30, the reporters, armed with new information for their editors in Boston, were set to board the towboats in Provincetown Harbor. However, the captains weren't. Another storm was ready to slam the area, and the captains opted to stay in port. "They were sworn at by every newspaper man who found time to indulge in the pastime, but the most these tow boat captains would do was to allow the newspapermen to sleep on board their vessels," the *Press* said.

The reporter from the *Press* somehow made it back to Portland by land, where he was lauded for his efforts. "He was the first newspaper man to walk along the surf-beaten, desolate coast from Race Point to Nauset, where the beach is strewn for miles with all that remains to tell the story of the lost steamer *Portland*," the *Press* said.

The *Boston Globe*'s two boats returned to Boston from their two-day Cape trip on November 30, with a reporter carrying "a package of news dispatches and also half a dozen letters. The latter were interested to his care by relatives of those who were lost with the *Portland*," the *Globe* reported on December 1. The letters were mailed to the families.

Through the trials and tribulations of the disaster, the media reporters received high praises, as Sylvester Baxter wrote the following year in *Scribner's Magazine*:

> *Except in actual warfare, the reporters and correspondents seldom encounter the exciting events they chronicle. But their work brings them close after, and in following the trails of disaster by land and sea, in spanning broken communications, and in getting their news back to the home office, they found in this widespread calamity an abundant field for the exercise of the hardy virtues.*

EPILOGUE

The terrible event rested so heavily on the hearts of many,
and will not soon depart.
—*Mrs. Annie Newcomb Spaulding of Greenwood, Massachusetts, from a*
composition written for her English class at age fifteen shortly after the storm,
published in the Provincetown Advocate, *December 1, 1938*

In his first sermon following the *Portland* Gale, the *Boston Globe* reported that Reverend W.I. Ward of the Center Methodist Church in Provincetown told his congregation that the previous Sunday was such a day as many never saw before—and all hope never to see again. "Tinged with Sadness" was the *Globe*'s headline.

Sadness certainly overtook the Rogers family of East Orleans during the months following the storm. Clarence Rogers, the twenty-year-old son of John G. Rogers, was walking along Nauset Beach in Orleans a few days after the storm when he spotted the body of a young girl washed ashore. Newspapers reported that it was the senior Rogers who found the girl, but a story told by Helen Freeman Stevens in the November 7, 1946 edition of the *Cape Codder* credited the son with the discovery. The *Bangor Daily Whig and Courier* reported these details on December 1, 1898:

> *The girl was not over twenty years of age. She had blue eyes, dark hair, light complexion and a full set of teeth. The body was clothed in underclothing, black corsets and a woolen jacket. On the little finger of the right hand was*

a ring which a stone in the center. The stone had been evidently washed away. The side setting of the ring was made of pearls.

Stunned, Clarence covered the girl's body with his coat and then headed back to town for the local undertaker's office.

The undertaker quickly took his cart to the beach, with Clarence riding along. As Stevens noted, "For some strange reason, perhaps because the victim was so near his own age, perhaps because the discovery had been his, the happening held for him a horrible fascination."

Back at the undertaker's office, while local officials scrambled to learn the girl's identity, a casket was chosen—by Clarence. "Well, if that is the way youth sees it, why not?" was their reasoning for accepting his choice.

However, finding any relatives was another matter. A detailed description was sent to newspapers in Boston and Portland, and after a while, relatives from Maine were headed for Orleans to claim the body. They weren't particularly fond of the casket choice that Clarence had made and chose another one.

Throughout the winter, Clarence stopped by the undertaker's office on occasion to "regretfully" view the casket. Later that winter, Clarence came down with a cold, which evolved into pneumonia.

"It was a hopeless case from the very first, although the doctor did all that he could," Stevens wrote. "Clarence died." The death notice in the February 25, 1899 edition of the *Yarmouth Register* offered these condolences: "Mr. and Mrs. Rogers, you have the deepest sympathy of the entire community in this your third deep and dark affliction."

Following his death, a choice for a casket had to be made. "All agreed that the coffin he had selected for the young victim of the wreck was the most appropriate one in which to be bury him," Stevens wrote. After placing Clarence's body in the tomb, two and a half miles from the family home, the family dog returned regularly, the *Register* reported:

> *Every day at a certain time the dog can be seen going up to the tomb, and there he lies down beside the door waiting for his master, "who cometh not out to meet his faithful friend." What a beautiful sight it is!*

Poetry and the *Portland*

The disaster also proved to be the inspiration behind a poem, "The Loss of Steamer *Portland*," which was written by Captain Frederick R. Eldredge and hydrographer George Eldridge of Chatham. The 326-word poem opens with the lines:

> *On the twenty-seventh of November,*
> *In the year of ninety-eight,*
> *A northeast blizzard swept the sea,*
> *Death following in its wake.*

The poem made several references to Hollis Blanchard, the *Portland*'s captain, who took the steamer to its doom. Memorial tributes to those lost were everywhere, and the two men made their creative contribution in January 1899.

"Hydrographer George Eldridge and Captain Frederick Eldredge, both citizens of this town, have each composed a poem entitled, 'The Loss of the Steamer *Portland*,'" the January 24, 1899 edition of the *Chatham Monitor* reported. "They are to be printed and offered for sale, we learn, by the principal news dealers of the country. We do not think that the two are in any way related, but both evidently have talents in the same direction."

The paper also wished the native poets much success. "Hydrographer Eldridge has a known reputation which will assist him in the sale of his work, while Captain F. Eldredge must depend largely on the merits of his production for financial returns," the *Monitor* said.

George Eldridge is credited with making the first charts of the Atlantic coast and began publishing the *Eldridge Tide and Pilot Book* in 1875.

The steamer *Portland* is shown here as a model during a 2021 exhibit at the Cape Cod Maritime Museum in Hyannis. *Author's collection.*

By the spring of 1899, music had been added to the mix. The *Monitor* reported on March 21, "Hydrographer Eldridge has composed music for his poem 'The Wreck of the *Portland*.' An accompaniment for the piano is to be added, when we have no doubt it will be printed and placed on sale."

The *Catalogue of Title Entries of Books and Other Articles* for that year listed music credit to Georgia French Perry, with words by Frederick R. Eldredge. That summer, the song made a particularly large impact on a visitor from New York. E.W. Blanchard, the *Portland* captain's brother, was staying at the Monomoyick Inn, according to the July 18, 1899 edition of the *Chatham Monitor*.

"[Blanchard] drove about town with George Eldridge," the paper said. "Mr. Eldridge sang to him the song of the *Portland*, which affected him very much."

It affected many more as well. As the poem concludes:

> *The news was spread the world around*
> *Through country and through city,*
> *Which fill the hearts of young and old*
> *With horror and with pity.*

Bibliography

Books

Bearse, Clarkson P., Sr. *The Tragedy of Monomoy Beach.* Harwich, MA: Goss Print, 1943.

Beston, Henry. *The Outermost House: A Year of Life on the Outer Beach of Cape Cod.* New York: Doubleday and Doran, 1928.

Biographical Sketches of Representative Citizens of the Commonwealth of Massachusetts. Boston: Graves and Steinbarger, 1901.

Blackington, A.H. *Yankee Yarns.* New York: Dodd, Mead and Company, 1954.

Catalogue of Title Entries of Books and Other Articles. Washington, D.C.: Library of Congress, Office of the Registry of Copyrights, 1899.

Clark, Captain Admont Gulick. *Sea Stories of Cape Cod and the Islands.* Orleans, MA: Lower Cape Publishing, 2000.

Dalton, J.W. *The Life-Savers of Cape Cod.* Boston: Barta Press, 1902.

Darling, Warren S. *The French Cable Station Museum: Orleans, Cape Cod, Massachusetts.* Orleans, MA: Lower Cape Publishing, 1988.

Digges, Jeremiah. *Cape Cod Pilot.* Provincetown, MA: Modern Pilgrim Press, 1937.

Egan, Leona Rust. *Provincetown as a Stage: Provincetown, The Provincetown Players, and the Discovery of Eugene O'Neill.* Orleans, MA: Parnassus Imprints, 1994.

Ellis, Ernest C. *Reminiscences of Ellisville.* Plymouth, MA: Memorial Press, 1973.

Fisher, Eric P. *Mighty Storms of New England.* Guilford, CT: Eric P. Fisher, Globe Pequot Books, 2021.

Freitas, Fred, and Dave Ball. *Warnings Ignored!: The Story of the Portland Gale—November 1898.* N.p.: self-published, 1995.

Millmore, Art. *And the Sea Shall Have Them All.* Weymouth, MA: self-published, 2019.

Pregot, Michael V. *Sea Captains of Cape Cod: Each Town's Contribution to Maritime History.* Boiling Springs, PA: Sunbury Press, 2022.

Richardson, Wyman. *The House on Nauset Marsh.* Woodstock, VT: Countryman Press, 2005.

Rich, Earle. *Cape Cod Echoes.* Wellfleet, MA: Earle Rich Memorial Scholarships Inc., 1973.

Samuels, Edward Augustus, and Henry Hastings Kimball. *Somerville, Past and Present: An Illustrated Historical Souvenir Commemorative of the Twenty-Fifth Anniversary of the Establishment of the City Government of Somerville, Massachusetts.* Somerville, MA: Samuels and Kimball, 1897.

Small, Isaac M. *Cape Cod Stories.* Buzzards Bay, MA: Lillian Small, 1934.

———. *Shipwrecks of Cape Cod.* Riverside, CT: Chatham Press, 1928.

Smith-Johnson, Robin. *Cape Cod Curiosities: Jeremiah's Gutter, the Historian Who Flew as Santa, Pukwudgies and More.* Charleston, SC: The History Press, 2018.

Snow, Edward Rowe. *New England Sea Tragedies.* New York: Dodd, Mead and Company, 1960.

———. *Storms and Shipwrecks of New England.* Carlisle, MA: Commonwealth Editions, 2003.

Sturdivant, Cyrus. *Sketches of the Life and Work of Captain Cyrus Sturdivant.* New York, 1879.

Tarbell, Arthur Wilson. *Cape Cod Ahoy!* Boston, MA: Little, Brown and Company, 1932.

Thoreau, Henry David. *Cape Cod.* New York: W.W. Norton and Company, 1951. Originally published in 1865.

Vorse, Mary Heaton. *Time and the Town: A Provincetown Chronicle.* New Brunswick, NJ: Rutgers University Press, 1991.

Wiseman, George W. *They Kept the Lower Lights Burning: The Story of the Seamen's Bethel at Martha's Vineyard, Massachusetts, and Its Chaplains.* Wilmore, KY: First Fruits Press, 2012.

Periodicals

Bangor Daily Whig and Courier. December 1, 1898.

Barnstable Patriot. January 12, 1895; December 5, 1898; October 31, 1904; April 28, 1919; September 13, 2002.

Boston Daily Advertiser. November 30, 1898; December 6 and 10, 1898.

Boston Globe. November 28–December, 1898; March 13, 1899.

Boston Journal. December 30, 1928.

Boston Post. November 28, 1898.

The Bulletin (Ontario, CA). October 7, 2008.

Cape Codder (Orleans, MA). November 7, 1946; December 6, 1956; November 30, 1961.

Cape Cod Item & Bee. December 6, 1898.

Cape Cod Magazine. 1921.

Cape Cod Standard-Times. January 1, 1967.

Cape Cod Times. April 15, 1989.

Chatham Monitor. November 30, December 6, December 13, 1898; January 13 and 24, 1899; March 21, 1899; July 18, 1899.

Denver Republican. February 1911.

East Hampton (NY) Star. November 26, 1998.

Falmouth Enterprise. December 10, 1898; 1931; December 14, 1933; August 15, 1939.

Harwich Independent. November 29, 1898.

Hyannis Patriot. March 29, 1909.

Los Angeles Herald. December 1, 1898.

Marshfield Mariner. June 9, 2010.

Martha's Vineyard Times. March 21, 2018; October 26, 2019.

Monthly Weather Review. U.S. Weather Bureau. January 1899.

Newsletter of the Dennis Historical Society, Dennis, Massachusetts. December 1987.

New York Journal. November 30–December 1, 1898.

New York Maritime Register. December 1898.

Old Farmer's Almanac. 1898.

Portland Daily Press. November 28–December 1898.

Prologue Magazine (Winter 2006). National Archives, Washington D.C.

Provincetown Advocate. November 29, December 6, 1898; September 12, 1929; October 15, 1931; September 10, 1933; December 1, 1938; December 16, 1948; December 20, 1951; December 8, 1962; November 13, 1969; November 25, 1971.

The Register. January 20, 1983.

Rockland (ME) Courier-Gazette. December 3, 1898.

Sandwich (MA) Independent. November 29–December 6, 1898.

Sandwich Observer. November 29, 1898; March 14, May 2, 1899, 1911.

Scribner's Magazine. November 1899.

Standard-Times (New Bedford, MA). November 29, 1998.

Vineyard Gazette. November 29, 1898.

Yankee Magazine. November 1966.

Yarmouth Register. January 3, 1891; November 29, 1898; February 25, 1899; March 19, 1910; May 10, 1919; July 15, 1938; June 19, 1941.

Interviews

Lindholm, Rick. Correspondence with the author. Eastham, MA, December 2015.

Mott, Glenn, and Sheila Mott. Correspondence with the author. Wrentham, MA, 2019.

Rongner, Yngve. Eastham Historical Society, June 1963.

Reports and Presentations

Bragg, Miriam C. "Shipwreck of the *Mary A. Tyler*—Off Paine's Creek—November 1898." Brewster Historical Society, May 1971.

Cape Cod National Seashore. "Historic Furnishings Report: Old Harbor Lifesaving Station." 2005.

MacMillan, Donald. "The Life Saving Service of Cape Cod: A Talk and Slides by Admiral Donald B. MacMillan." Undated. Provincetown History Project.

Shepherd, Douglas H. "The Gale of November 1898." Excerpts from a radio speech by the keeper of Wood End Lighthouse, Provincetown, MA, 1928. Provincetown History Project.

Snow, Al. Summary of the *Portland* Gale for the Eastham Historical Society, 1961.

U.S. Life-Saving Service Annual Report, 1899.

Wolfe, Robert J., and T.J. Ferguson. "Traditional Cultural Property Assessment: Dune Shacks of the Peaked Hill Bars Historic District Cape Cod National Seashore." May 2006.

Websites

Massachusetts Board of Underwater Archaeological Resources. https://www.mass.gov/orgs/board-of-underwater-archaeological-resources.
Stellwagen Bank National Marine Sanctuary. https://stellwagen.noaa.gov.

Letters

Letter found in the Pratt Papers at Freeman Farm, Sandwich, November 30, 1898, addressed to "Mr. Pratt." Benjamin Haines, Sandwich Town Archives, Sandwich Public Library, Sandwich, MA.

Index

Y

About the Author

Since the start of the millennium, Don Wilding has been telling stories of Cape Cod Outer Beach history. An award-winning writer and editor for Massachusetts newspapers for thirty-six years, Don is the author of three other books: *Henry Beston's Cape Cod: How* The Outermost House *Inspired a National Seashore*, *A Brief of History of Eastham: On the Outer Beach of Cape Cod* and *Shipwrecks of Cape Cod: Stories of Tragedy and Triumph*. He has worked as a tour guide and lecturer and has taught local history classes for adults on the Outer Cape. Don and his wife, Nita, live in Franklin, Massachusetts, and in Dennis on Cape Cod.

dwCapeCod.com
donwilding@gmail.com